The Impact

Achieving success in your business

To your Success – Don't ever quit

Stephan Longworth

imageplus publishing

imageplus
publishing

Published by
Imageplus publishing
PO Box 458,
Macclesfield, Cheshire SK10 2WY
Telephone: +44 (0)845 607 6724
info@imageplus.org.uk
www.imageplus.org.uk

Second Edition: 2013 Stephan Longworth
ISBN 978-0-9570506-1-7

About the author

Stephan Longworth was born and raised on a south Manchester council estate. He had a comprehensive school education, then studied Engineering at Stockport College of Technology. He worked in aviation as a marshaller/airside safety officer and trainer.

Stephan is a student of success, and over the last 17 years has risen steadily to the top in the Network Marketing industry. His driving force is helping others to reach their true potential.

Stephan is currently a National Group Leader with the Utility Warehouse, one of the largest and most successful companies in the Network Marketing industry. He has built a team with in excess of 61,000 customers (at the time of writing), and an annual turnover of several millions of pounds a year. He enjoys a lifestyle he once only dreamed of.

He is a respected speaker, with a unique style that not only inspires and motivates his audience, but that also delivers practical tools that help people achieve success.

This is the Stephan's first book, now in its second edition.

Acknowledgements and dedication

I have gathered the information in this book - unscientifically - over years and years from countless people, countless places. I owe my knowledge and understanding to the advice and insights of many people who have given generously of their time, patience and energy to initiate me into, and educate me in, the mysteries of business, life and this amazing industry of ours; Network Marketing.

I was tutored by some of the best in the business, National Network Leaders Clive Leach and Diana Ross, who have one of the largest, most stable and profitable businesses in the industry. If it wasn't for their driving force and tenacity, I would not be where I am now.

To all the authors, contributors, teachers, friends and acquaintances who have helped me; my thanks.

And, where appropriate; my apologies!

I would also like to thank:

Joan, Joe, Carol, Kieron, Graham, Louise, Peter, Paul, Robin, Wes, Jimmy, Gary, Chris, Steve.

The Company executives, the Hon. Charles Wigoder, Andrew Lindsay -MBE and Olympic Gold medallist, Sydney 2000.

Credits and special thanks to:

Angela Brady-D'Souza; your keen eye was invaluable. Only a dear friend would take the time to read through many rough drafts of this book.

Alan Hamilton from Imageplus publishing, for all your hard work and patience.

Humphrey Couchman, who edited both editions of this book. Your editorial skills and knowledge were an invaluable asset to this project. Thank you for your helpful insights and suggestions, thanks for believing in me and in the value of this work.

Finally, thanks to **Wayne Coupland**, for your help and support; not only to myself but the entire network. Your respect for the Distributors in our business is infectious; you are both an inspiration and a friend.

With love, I dedicate this book to:

Dad, Mum, Barrie and **Sam.**

To **Ashley** and **Jamie**, the finest sons anyone could ever hope to have, sons that have been so forgiving over the years, sons whose hearts are bigger than the bodies that carry them... thank you.

Georgia, my fabulous wife

Mere thanks cannot express my gratitude to my wife, Georgia, for her encouragement, support, love and belief in me. Georgia, you have been my oak tree, my rock; I can never fully repay you.

Thousands of people join Network Marketing in the UK each year. The Utility Warehouse is the UK's most successful Network Marketing business, and Stephan Longworth is one of the Company's most successful Distributors. When you are new to this business, you need the correct mindset, and to make sure you get started in the right way. The **IMPACT SYSTEM** ™ will help you on both scores.

Read this book, follow the system, and you're on the road to success

"I have a passion to help team members achieve success in their Utility Warehouse business." - Stephan Longworth

"Stephan Longworth is a remarkable leader in the Network Marketing industry. When Diana and I first met Stephan, it was obvious that he had a massive desire to succeed. Over the years he has been like a sponge, soaking up ideas, concepts and strategies and has exhibited the work ethic required to create and build a large, dynamic network of authorised independent Distributors. It has been and still is a privilege to have Stephan and his wife, Georgia, as great colleagues and true friends."

Clive Leach and Diana Ross,

National Network Leaders and Authorised Distributors

Contents

Foreword

Dear friend,

Congratulations and welcome!

You might be about to begin a journey towards creating a business of lasting success, a business you truly deserve. You might already be on that journey.

Either way, I have huge respect for what you are doing.

I have been there, and I know how it feels. I joined the Utility Warehouse – or Telecom Plus as it was then – some years ago. No other business in Britain offers everyone such an opportunity to start with nothing but a dream and become financially free. It treats each person with equal respect.

Be mindful that you should be your own best customer. Remember when you bring a new person into your team, to ensure that they get some customers or no one gets paid!

I started, like everyone else does, at the bottom. But with drive, effort and dogged determination, I have climbed our 'stairway to success'.

For several years now, I have been passionately pursuing the answers to these questions: What shapes our behaviour? What shapes our success? How can we create lasting change within ourselves? How can we create lasting change within others?

Through my studies, from seminars, books and CDs, from my mistakes and successes, and from my interaction over the years with an incredibly diverse group of people — from full-time parents to professional athletes, from teachers and trainers to high-ranking police officers, from blue-collar workers to top-flight executives — I have combined tools and strategies which have helped me maximise my capabilities.

I have long envisioned the creation of a system; one where new Distributors can immediately apply themselves and make profound changes in the quality of their lives, by building successful businesses.

And now I feel genuinely excited, passionate and privileged, to have the opportunity to share with you the best of what I have learned.

I call it 'The Impact System^{TM}'.

The success of all of our Distributorships is shaped by what we know, what we believe, by our habits and by our skills.

The Impact System^{TM} has given me, and now can give you, the opportunity to take control of these forces, and design your business exactly the way you want it to be. You will acquire the skills, knowledge and strategies necessary to make your ambitions come true.

The Impact System^{TM} can help you take control and change the quality of your business, and your life, forever.

You'll learn methods and techniques that I discovered over many years.

There are many ways to be successful in Network Marketing. But I have found that some ways are better than others. I'd like to share them with you.

And through it all, you will develop the skills you need to become a leader in this business.

Accept the opportunities ahead with enthusiasm, and your business will prosper.

But always remember this; the Impact System™ is built around you taking the simple actions, on a daily basis, that will reward you the most. In business, activity always comes before results. Income follows correct activity.

This business is built on the laws of business, not the laws of the casino. This is not a game of chance. You must understand that there are skills you need to learn to be successful.

My goal in developing the Impact System™ is to provide the best support possible to every Distributor. If you are without immediate upline support, this programme can be the success coach you're looking for.

If you have great upline support, this programme will complement that, and make you better.

I understand that everybody who enters this business has different amounts of time, energy, self-confidence, desire and talent. That's one of the reasons I have made the Impact System™ adaptable to every Distributor, from the novice to the more experienced.

When I designed the Impact System™, I had in mind a Distributor investing one to two hours per day into his or her business. But you can adjust it down, if you have less time to put in, or you can adjust it up, if you have more ambitious goals.

Life produces extraordinary rewards for those who give in extraordinary ways. Let's make a commitment today to participate together with intensity and passion, let's go beyond anything we've done before. Let's start the process of taking our business – and our lives – to the next level. Let's start NOW!

Above all, this book is meant to help the men and women joining this great business; those many thousands of people who still dare to dream big, who believe in enterprise and being their own boss. In these troubled economic times, many have begun to question themselves, and our country. You won't find such fears haunting Utility Warehouse Distributors. We will keep the flame alive when so many others have lost hope.

Believe in the abilities you possess and give yourself the necessary time to get the results you desire.

Start right where you are... but start.

Best wishes, and respect,

Stephan.

Heart and soul – who and what I am

Writing a book is a big undertaking, especially if you've never done it before. *The Impact System* is my first book, and I'm very proud that this is the second edition.

Quite a few people told me that I didn't put enough about me, my story, in the first edition. So that's what this section is. It's about who and what I am.

I hope it will show you why I believe in Network Marketing, and why I put my heart and soul into it, every day.

My story begins in a not-so-affluent area of a rough council housing estate in South Manchester. I joke that it was so rough even the dogs used to go round the estate in twos! I came from a poor family – my dad was an engineer – and I didn't like it. We never seemed to have enough money for anything but the bare essentials. I had a lot of hand me down clothes, that sort of thing.

My Mum and Dad were loving, but they didn't do money very well. From a young age, I wanted to know why it was that some people were more successful than others, had nicer cars and bigger houses. Something deep inside me said there must be a reason for this.

I left school with no real qualifications. I was a child who had difficulty reading, and I was labelled a bit 'slow' in junior school. I was in the half of the class that made the top half possible. One particular teacher reminded me of that on a regular basis (teachers could get away with lots of stuff in the 60's). On one particular day, he pulled me to the front of the class and battered me, because I was 'giving him cheek'. Believe me, that teacher was a big man who didn't hold back. If my life-long friend, Kieron, hadn't jumped in and stopped him, who knows what would have happened.

Wasn't that an empowering way to teach?

That started my major dislike for school. It seemed I was always getting into trouble of some kind or other. I got more detentions than other kids. I wasn't academic, and failed my 11+.

But even at a young age, I did have a knack for fixing things. I fixed other kids' bicycles, the neighbours' lawn mowers, I sharpened their shears, etc. I made a bit of pocket money.

I also made people laugh, which helped me build rapport with them.

I became more popular at secondary school. I was good at metalwork and art and craft. When I left school I went into engineering and got an apprenticeship. That seemed my destiny; my Dad was an engineer, his Dad had been an engineer, and my brother Barrie was a very gifted engineer.

I scraped into Stockport College of Technology; in 1974, they would take anyone! For the first few months of my new engineering career, I was a spectacular failure. In a class of 45 student engineers, I was number 45 every month. Although I did move up a couple of places to number 43, after two other boys quit the course!

All that changed when my Dad grabbed me by the scruff of the neck one day and offered me some pearls of wisdom that remain with me today.

He said, "Son, if you want to get on in life, go out there, study successful people, and copy their behaviour."

I did take that advice on board. I used to play pool and drink beer with the college lecturers and some of the young men at the end of their City & Guilds apprenticeships, in a pub called the Nelson Tavern. It's still there, on the corner of Greek Street and the A6 in Stockport.

I befriended and built rapport with these people. And, to my surprise, they were very helpful in advising me about what I should be doing. Some of the college lecturers even gave up personal time to help me.

My attitude changed. I applied myself, worked hard, and just 48 short months later I qualified top of my class with distinction. I am still proud of that today.

I used the same philosophy when I entered aviation; copy people who are good at what they do; borrow their ideas. Why try to reinvent the wheel?

I did OK in airside safety, working on the runways and taxiways at Manchester airport for 14 years. But things were changing in my life. It seemed like all the rules were changing. Going to work on a Monday wasn't as inspiring as it had once been. We were living beyond our income; too much month at the end of the money. We had two children, a dog, goldfish... So I decided to look at other ways to make money. I bought and sold cars. I invested in the stock market. But that didn't go too well! In fact, I lost all our money, and even our house.

Then I found Network Marketing.

Why did I get involved in Network Marketing? Because the start-up cost was low, it was low risk and, with effort, had huge potential. And they would take me!

I used the same philosophy in the Network Marketing industry that I used in engineering and aviation; build trust and rapport, study successful people, study winners, study people who are good at what they do, and copy them.

I went to a Network Marketing seminar years ago. The speaker was 71 years of age. He spoke in broken English with a strong Spanish accent. He had worked all his life as a factory worker, and he told us why he joined Network Marketing: after one year of retirement at 66, he and his wife were running out of money. But after five years working in Network Marketing, with consistent and persistent effort, he was making 10k a month! That blew my mind. I asked myself; how could a retired factory worker who could just about string a sentence together in English do that?

He also spoke about why people lose and why people win in life. He said, "Winners do the things losers are unwilling to do." He also said that the fact we were at that seminar put us in the top 10% of successful people in society (a great 'ego stroke' on his part!).

That seminar changed my thinking.

When the meeting was over and everyone else had gone to the bar, he was packing all his stuff away. I introduced myself to him, and asked how a person like me, who had been in engineering and airside safety, who had never done sales or marketing, how could someone like me join and make the kind of passive income he was making?

He said to me, "Big man, you want to make big money in this industry?"

I said that would be nice.

He then walked me to the back of the room and pushed me against the wall. He said, "Will you represent the length of this

18

room as one year, no-turn-back effort? Not to look over your shoulder left, not look over your shoulder right and not look behind you. Will you do that?"

I said, "I think I can do that."

He said, "No, big man. Yes or no."

I said, "Yes. For that kind of money, I am willing to do whatever it takes."

"That is good, big man, I can teach you no more," and he left me stood against the wall!

Big lesson. You never know what it might be; a seminar, a book, a thought here or there, encouragement, especially at a trying time (and rest assured, I have had plenty of those in this business), the little things that add up.

It was at that event that I caught the vision of Network Marketing. I understood the dynamics of passive and reoccurring income, and the value of creating an ongoing income. That night, I got excited again about the dreams and goals that I had for my life. I didn't realise the journey would take me all over the place, meeting some truly amazing and wonderful people, while building a team of thousands of Distributors.

I didn't know the decision I made that night would eventually help me and my family to have all the material things we had barely dared to dream of.

But success can be an elusive animal. It didn't happen quickly at first, and after 18 months in the Telecom Plus business our cheque was around £120 per month. The business wasn't going very fast and, to be honest, I was still only thinking that it would give us some extra money. I still didn't see that it would give us our dreams.

All that changed when I had the good fortune to be invited to the Midland Hotel in Manchester, to meet a gentleman called Charles Wigoder, who was then Chief Executive of Telecom Plus.

Charles changed my perspective on everything. He gave me the vision to see how things could be.

I shudder to think what my life would be like if I hadn't had that meeting. Life has its turning points and that certainly was a big one for me.

I made a decision that day to do whatever it takes.

That was some years ago. Since then, I have done whatever it takes. It hasn't been easy – friends and family thought I was barking at the moon – but I have built a big business, one of the biggest in the UK. I have put my heart and soul into it, every day. I have observed successful people and copied them. I have worked hard, and consistently.

And yes, I am reaping the rewards now in terms of income, and opportunity, and freedom. My life today is a million miles away from where it might have been, thanks to this incredible business.

So that's a little of me. That's my story. Now it's up to you to write yours.

Decide what you want from our business, find out how I and others have succeeded, and then do the same things we have done. You will achieve the same results we have, over time.

The secret of success is so simple in this business. That's not to say it's easy, but it is simple. You will get whatever you want from this business if you want it badly enough, if you are willing to persist long and hard enough.

It doesn't matter if you are black, white, old or young, rich or poor, well educated or not so well educated. You can determine what you get out by what you put in. How cool is that?

The proof is all around us. Everywhere you look in the Utility Warehouse there are success stories, men and women from every walk of life and background.

I know this works because I have tested and proven the system. What I have learned along the way I have written in this book.

I have taught the Impact System to thousands of people, and it has worked for them too.

It can work for you.

PART 1

GET YOUR HEAD RIGHT

Mindset

Mindset or attitude is going to be a major factor in the success or failure of your business.

Your mindset is your fuel.

A positive mental attitude is about not living in a fantasy world, but facing reality; with anticipation, not apprehension.

What you are today is the sum of all your past attitude and thoughts. And that means that if you can change your thoughts and mindset today, you can change your future.

You know the old saying, 'Is the glass half empty or half full?'

How do you see things, positively or negatively? Do you look for a positive outcome in situations or do you look for a negative outcome?

In the simplest terms, a good mindset is wanting to do the best you can.

It's emotional!

People act on things based on how they feel.

Our emotional side is what makes us do some things and not others. How you feel about this business is going to have a huge impact on your success.

How you feel about other things is also really important. But - you can learn how to adapt your feelings to help you succeed.

1. Who can change the past?

All of us come into this business with our own unique past; past successes, past failures, past relationships, past disappointments and all of our past experiences.

You can treat your past in two ways.

You can use your past as a stick, to beat yourself over the head with, saying, "If only I had done this," or "If only I had done that, my life would be so much better today". Some people spend their entire lives replaying the past.

The past is not where you want to spend your time.

Here's a better way to treat your past. Use it as a school, a vast resource to learn from and to better yourself with. You got a result from everything you did in the past. It might have been good, or it might have been bad, it doesn't matter; you got a result. From that result you can learn more than you might imagine, to improve your life in the future. Simply study the result and refine your future actions.

Treat your past as a school. You've paid for that education and no one can take it from you! If it's been a harsh education, you can rejoice today, because through that experience, you've become more valuable. It's not the easy times that make you grow.

A good way to look at the past is to take all your years and the knowledge you've gained from them, and invest all of that into this upcoming year.

Today is the first day of your future, not another day of your past. Let today be the day you decide to take your past and use it to create the future you deserve.

2. What about the future?

The future is an awesome force that you can apply to today's activity.

Why did you join this business? Why are you reading this book?

Not for an immediate result. You're doing it for the future! You can take a well designed future and the inspiration that gives you to find the time and energy to succeed in this business.

I call the future 'the promise'. Now there's a price to pay for that promise, but it's easier to pay when the promise is strong. Plan your future well, and it can become the greatest pull on your life. Any time you are struggling and feeling discouraged, use the promise of your future to help you pay the price you need to today.

On the other hand, if the promise is weak, the price is almost impossible to pay. If you can't see the meaning in your daily activities, if they're not pulling you towards your well planned future, the price can become too much to bear.

So make your future and its pull on you a strong one. It will carry you through almost any adversity.

The key to this is Goal-Setting, which we will look at a little later.

3. What about others?

You won't succeed by yourself. We all need other people. We need each other's ideas. We need each other's inspiration. We need each other's strength. We need each other's encouragement. If you think you can succeed without other people, you're mistaken.

But that's not a sign of weakness.

When you understand how valuable other people are is when you become powerful.

4. How about ME?

Understanding self-worth is fundamental to your accelerated progress.

I don't know you, but I know something about you; you have greatness within you.

You have the ability to do things that you can't even imagine. You have talents and skills within you that you haven't even begun to reach yet.

It's not important to change how other people view us; what's important is how we view ourselves.

Look at yourself. What could you do? What do you think is your highest potential?

Decide today not to allow other people's negative or mediocre expectations of you become reality. If other people don't expect great things from you, then understand your own self-worth and expect great things from yourself.

Jim Rohn, a man I admire enormously, said:

Jim Rohn, a man I admire enormously, said:

"The only limitation placed on our abilities is our inability to easily recognise our unlimited nature. It takes effort to become aware of our staggering and limitless abilities. It takes effort to become enthusiastic over a cause; it takes effort to continue when our results, as well as our friends, tell us to give up trying.

It does not, however, take effort to fail. It requires little else than a slowly deteriorating attitude about our present, our future, and ourselves.

It is ironic that one of the few things in this life over which we have total control is our own attitudes, and yet most of us live our entire life behaving as though we had no control whatsoever. By our attitude, we decide to read or not to read. By our attitude, we decide to try or give up. By our attitude, we blame ourselves for our failure or we foolishly blame others. Our attitude determines whether we love or hate, tell the truth or lie, act or procrastinate, advance or recede, and by our own attitude, we, and we alone, actually decide whether to succeed or fail."

Internal sabotage

We need to share some of the things that can hurt you, as well as the things that will help you. It's important to understand the threats we all face, and how to conquer them.

1. Lethargy

Lethargy is the sluggish approach to life. Lethargy is that shrug of the shoulder saying, "I can't be bothered."

I tell you this; if you really can't be bothered, then you won't do it.

So get bothered! Get bothered about your future! Get bothered about your life! Strong feelings are what I'm after.

I am often asked, "What type of people do you want in your team?" or "What type of people do you like to be around?" My answer is always, "People with strong feelings.'

I don't even care what they feel strongly about, as long as they feel strongly about it, because strong feelings will always triumph over lethargy.

Feel strongly.

2. Indecision

Indecision is mental paralysis. Indecision can bring you to your knees. Indecision is when a person says, "I know I'm on the fence but I don't know what to do."

Indecision is the thief of opportunity, time and happiness.

You have to make decisions. It makes no difference what side they're on. What makes a difference is learning the habit of making decisions. A life full of adventure, a life full of success, is a life full of many decisions.

Make the decision and move on.

Learn to decide.

3. Doubt

The worst doubt that a person can have in their life is self-doubt. To have no confidence in themselves.

If you doubt for a period of time, pretty soon you'll get good at doubting. A person can become a practised doubter, and I'll tell you what happens then. You end up with an empty cup, or empty pockets.

The only healthy doubt is the one that is really wanting an answer.

Remember this. Trust is better than doubt. Belief is better than questioning.

I'm not saying that you're going to win with that formula every time, but you'll win with it a lot more than you'll win with doubt. And you'll be happier in the process.

Choose belief over doubt.

4. Stress and worry

Stress can cause you problems; health problems, social problems, personal problems, economic problems.

Remember this. The heavy chains of worry are forged in idle hours.

Repeat. The heavy chains of worry are forged in *idle hours*.

So get busy, and remember that most of what you get stressed about never happens.

Don't worry.

5. Being over cautious

This is the timid approach to life. Some people are always waiting for better days to come.

But better days won't just turn up. You have to take the days as they are and make them into what you want them to be.

There has never been a better day than today.

One of the biggest fears people have is What if; "What if this happens? What if that happens?" People who fail will always focus on the risk within the opportunity.

People who succeed look at the opportunity within the risk. You can't get away from risk. Nobody goes through life without risk.

Do you think you can have success and happiness without risk? Impossible! Risk is part of our lives. Understand that, accept it, and don't be afraid.

Accept risk.

6. Pessimism

The pessimist always looks on the dark side. The pessimist always looks at why this business won't work. The pessimist doesn't look for virtue. They look for faults and if they find a fault they start to enjoy it.

Pessimists see themselves as smarter than the rest, but they lose the good in life as a result.

The good in life is there for the optimists among us to enjoy.

Be optimistic.

7. Whinging and moaning

Whinging and moaning will get you nowhere. People who whinge and moan are much better served by taking the energy they use to whinge and moan and applying it to constructive or positive action. This would actually get them some results!

If you spend your time complaining, you're wasting time you could be using for much better things.

Don't complain.

The importance of goals

A good attitude alone will not make you a success.

If you're driving somewhere and you have the wrong map, or your sat nav has the wrong information in it, a good attitude will just help you get lost with a smile on your face!

A good attitude alone is not enough. You must also have a clear picture of where you're headed. Your plan must consist of clear, specific goals that will help you reach your ultimate goal.

Imagine that your ultimate goal is a holiday in Monte Carlo. Your plan is to drive from where you are to Monte Carlo. Your specific goals are to drive 200 miles a day and in your head is a picture of every stop you will make between here and Monte Carlo.

That's goal-setting.

Try this goal-setting exercise. Try it now:

Write down a clear goal and four good reasons why you believe you will achieve it.

My clear specific goal is:

....

The reasons why I will achieve my clear specific goal are:

1...

2...

3...

4...

List the obstacles you need to overcome to accomplish these goals.

....

....

List the solutions to these obstacles; include the people who can help you.

....

....

List the action steps you need to take each day to achieve your goals, and the date you wish to accomplish them by.

Steps: ....

....

....

....

The date I will achieve this goal is...

Your signature...

Now, just like the holiday in Monte Carlo, you know where you want to go, and you have the map to tell you how to get there.

Your attitude will help drive you to your personal goals.

Your attitude will help you reap the benefits of achieving your goals.

Your attitude will help you overcome every obstacle and challenge that stands between you and your goals.

Your attitude will help you to take action when it would be easier not to.

And always remember: your attitude today is the foundation of your future.

IBEs and Dream-Stealers

When you start any new business venture you will come across the IBEs (Instant Bloody Experts) and Dream-Stealers. They are the cynics, the people who tell you this can't be done. They may even laugh at you, or ridicule you.

People will be negative with you, that's just the way it is. But remember this; a dog doesn't bark at a parked car. You're moving now, and people will bark their negative opinions at you. Are you mentally strong enough to resist them?

These are the kind of people who know everything in life. They always have to be right or they've done it bigger and better than you. If you've just jumped out of a plane at 15,000ft to raise money for a good cause, they jumped from 25,000ft without the aid of a parachute and oxygen... or if you have run a marathon, they did it quicker.

If you tell them about the benefits of our business or services they will rudely interrupt you and say something like, "It's a Scam, it's a pyramid, I can get it cheaper."

These people are here to try and question your belief. You must be strong and resist their ignorance.

I have the good fortune to visit the USA a few times a year. One time, in Florida, I saw a brand new gun-metal grey Bugatti Veyron Grand Sport parking at a shopping mall. A well dressed, tall, handsome man got out of the driving seat. I asked him if it was OK to have a look inside his car. He said 'no problem', and even let me have a look under the bonnet. Turns out he was a successful young lawyer, and a nice guy.

Georgia turned to me and said, "Don't you just love a winner?"

A few months later, I was in Manchester with some friends on a night out, when we spotted a brand new Porsche with a young-looking man driving it. The husband of one of my friends turned and said, "I wonder which poor ba**ard he ripped off to get that car?"

It's sad. Some people love winners, some people just want to tear them down.

I remember my first big hurdle with this, like it was yesterday.

I was so excited about the business opportunity, and I genuinely thought everyone else would be excited too. How wrong I was.

I jumped in with both feet and did my first "home meeting". I invited a friend called Larry and several other airport colleagues to come to my house at 8pm one evening.

We had gone to the trouble of getting cakes, crisps, nuts and dips. We'd made sandwiches. We'd bought wine, beer and spirits.

8pm came and went. 9pm came and went. 10pm came and went. They had all let me down. And they didn't even have the courtesy to call and let me know.

I went to bed that night fat and drunk.

When I woke up the next morning, I contemplated quitting. But I didn't.

When I went to work, the people who should have been at my home that evening gave me a wide birth. It wasn't until sometime later that I found out that it was Larry who had poisoned their minds. He had convinced them it wasn't worth it, that they shouldn't go. They'd believed him. He stole their dreams and he damn near stole mine too.

You will have Larry's in your life. Most of us do.

Don't let the dream-stealers get the better of you. Stay on track; focus on your belief, follow the system.

I am a product of the System, the books, CD's and events.

I know it works.

Self-belief

I can give you all the tools and encouragement in the world but if you don't have self belief you will be like a cork in the stormy ocean of life, bobbing up and down with no direction

Self-belief is the guiding compass that leads us toward our goals and gives us the certainty to know we will get there.

Without belief, or the ability to tap into it, people can be totally defeated. With powerful guiding belief, you can see what you want and you are motivated to get it.

You'll know the saying, 'I'll believe it when I see it.' I say that you must believe it *before* you can see it. That goes for any endeavour in life.

The more I learn about human behaviour, the more I learn about the extraordinary power that belief has over our lives.

A classic example of the power of belief is the four-minute mile.

Before 1954, the consensus was that it was impossible to run a mile in under four minutes. Many scientists and doctors said it was physically impossible. The athletics world proclaimed that it could not be done.

But one man believed he could do it.

On 6 May 1954, Dr. Roger Bannister ran a mile in three minutes, 59.4 seconds.

Aside from being an incredible achievement, what is really interesting about this is that within a couple of weeks, six other athletes also ran a mile in under a minute. Within a month, eight others had achieved the same.

How did this happen?

Simply because the athletes who followed Bannister stopped believing that it was impossible and started believing it was possible. History is littered with examples of achievements stemming from great belief; from aviation and space travel, to medical advances and ground-breaking technology.

The moment you start believing your goals, ambitions and dreams are possible, they become possible.

Self-belief is powerful. If you believe you can or if you believe you can't do something... you're right.

Your desire and belief system

Your desire is the runway from which you take off for your goals and ambitions.

Your belief is the compass that keeps you on course.

Self-limiting beliefs

You may have a desire to be more successful, to make more money, or to have better personal relationships, but the reality is that without a well formed desire and belief system, self-limiting beliefs will make you crash.

You cannot ignore your self-limiting beliefs. They have been with you a long time, since childhood in many cases. Self-limiting beliefs lead to a negative self-image, a self-image that you did not create.

An example of a self-limiting belief:

Suppose you were asked to walk across a plank of wood, 40 feet long, three feet wide and one foot thick. It is lying on the ground and you are asked to walk from one end to the other without falling off.

Could you do that? Of course you could.

But now the same plank of wood is being used as a bridge between two very high buildings. Could you now walk along the plank? In reality, probably not.

But ask yourself this: has the plank changed in any way?

Obviously, the answer is no.

So what would stop you? The answer is, lack of belief and too much imagination. You imagine, for example; it's too high, I'll slip off, I might get hurt, I'll die!

You imagine all sorts of self-limiting beliefs.

But just as lack of belief and imagination built up your self-limiting beliefs, then belief and imagination can be used to bring them down. And you need to! As you well know, your-self limiting beliefs are real enough, and they will prevent you from achieving your goals.

Fixed beliefs

As well as self-limiting beliefs, we also have fixed beliefs.

Fixed beliefs are primarily the result of our personal history, background and life experience. As both self-limiting beliefs and fixed beliefs are initially formed in childhood, it is important to look at our early years in order to understand them.

Most children learn in two main ways:

1. By imitation.

2. By moving from an uncomfortable experience towards a comfortable experience.

Our very early awareness is that we are helpless and need those closest to us – probably our parents – to give us assistance, love, affection and protection.

We learn to gain the attention of others by moving, and making noises. When we're hungry, we cry until we're fed. When we want affection, we cry until somebody comes and picks us up.

While these actions usually achieve the result we want, they also reinforce the fact that we are dependent.

All of this happened to you. Over the next few years, like most children, you probably dribbled, had trouble with your bowel functions, ate chaotically, etc. All of this was witnessed by many people, whose reactions confirmed to you that as well as being dependent, you were now also grubby, with sticky hands and socially unacceptable.

By the age of four you had probably, to a large degree, developed speech, some mastery of a knife and fork, learned to run and, in general, made great progress.

Far from receiving consistent and generous praise from all of those closest to you, they presented you with the next ordeal in your life... school!

So there you were, merrily trotting off to school. This was the new start.

So what happened?

The older children were smarter, more co-ordinated, better educated and less helpless and, possibly worst of all, they were bigger. You know that's true because they told you so.

So another film of negative self-image formed. This pattern continued throughout your youth and teenage years, until the day you finally left home to 'make your own way'.

The only problem was that as you grew up and got bigger and older, your negative self-image tagged along with you like a shadow...

Our negative self-image has a few key weapons, including the fear of failure and the fear of rejection. These are formed by our exposure to criticism at an early age, which leads us to develop negative habits.

How real is this fear? Very real! And it has been with you a long time.

But you can look at fear in another way:

- **F**alse
- **E**vidence
- **A**ppearing
- **R**eal

According to experts, we are born with just two fears: the fear of loud noises and the fear of falling. That's why children at a very tender age can put their hand in an open flame!

All our other fears we have picked up and brought with us through life.

Now, there are good fears in life and there are destructive fears.

The good fears are about self-preservation; fear of falling, fear of a loud noise or explosion, fear of drowning, fear of fire. These are good fears.

But we also have self-limiting fears; fear of what others think of us, fear of rejection, fear of the unknown, fear of failure, fear of success. These are destructive fears.

What to do about fear? Meet it head on.

Can fear be avoided? The problem with avoiding fear is that it gives credibility to the fear, and will also increase the habitual nature of it.

For example; many people, conditioned from an early age, are afraid of the dark. So they try to avoid the dark, and they sleep with the light on. This gives them temporary relief, but does not address the fear itself, and so it gradually leads to greater fear.

A genuine antidote to fear is action.

Identify your fears and take action to stop them.

If you are fearful of walking under ladders, you walk around them. Take action, and stop walking round ladders!

If you avoid picking up the phone to make an appointment, that is the very action you must do to overcome your fear of the telephone. Pick up the phone, make the call. Make the appointment.

In just a short few calls you will become better at it.

Ralph Waldo Emerson said, "Do what you fear most and the death of fear is certain."

You will either face the fear of doing the business or you will face the fear of not doing the business!

Attack the fear habit. Don't avoid your fears, confront them.

To be successful, you will need belief.

- Belief in yourself
- Belief in the Company and what it does
- Belief in this great industry, Network Marketing.

Positive thinking

Positive thinking, what I call 'realistic optimism', actually works!

The world in your mind is just as real as your external world. Negative thinking prevents you from being in control of your life, while positive thinking puts you in control. Control starts with thoughts, thoughts determine your feelings, and feelings determine your actions, as I discussed earlier.

The law of cause and effect says that every effect has a specific cause. Thoughts are causes.

You will destroy yourself if you continually have negative thoughts.

Think positively, and you will be unstoppable.

I have learned that most people believe that they can think whatever they wish, without consequences. It is not true. Whatever you consistently think about can eventually come true, whether it is positive or negative.

Always think positively.

Your goals

Your goals are a fundamental part of self-development, and of building a successful business. They are what will motivate you, and keep you motivated.

As we have seen, effective goal-setting is made up of two key elements:

1. Having a clear specific goal.

2. Identifying the actions that can help you achieve the goal.

Your goals, combined with an understanding of, and belief in, the actions that will get you there, are your motivation.

We will look at motivation in more detail later.

Personal inventory

This is a short list of assets you need to help achieve your goals. Rate yourself on a scale of one to ten (where ten is strongest) in each of the areas.

Once you determine your strengths and weaknesses, use the list of suggested reading and listening at the end of this book to improve areas where you face an obstacle.

- burning desire
- phone skills
- are you teachable
- drive/determination
- persistence
- confidence
- self reliance
- leadership skills
- commitment.

Excuses

I have heard all the excuses.

Whenever people quit the Utility Warehouse (and they do), they call or email me, and they say, "Steph, I'm quitting today and I want to tell you whose fault it is."

The email may complain that the individual's sponsor didn't train or work with them properly, or the starter pack didn't arrive on time, or the plan didn't work the way it was supposed to... believe me, I have heard them all.

So if in the future you are thinking that you might quit and you're struggling to come up with a reason, just call me and I'll give you an excuse to put in your email. How about: I'm too old, I'm too young, I'm not educated enough, I'm too educated, I don't have the time, nothing any good ever happens to me, I'm not smart enough, I don't have the right background.

I just wish people could be totally honest with me and send me an email that says, "Stephan, I'm quitting today because *that's what I do.* I've done it before and I'll do it again."

Dismantling the excuses

Let's have a quick look at three of the most common excuses I hear, and my answers to them:

Excuse: 'I am too old.' Hogwash! Colonel Sanders was 66 when he started Kentucky Fried Chicken.

Excuse: 'I'm not smart enough.' Baloney! The great majority of the world's most successful people left school with very little formal academic education. It's about attitude, not exam results.

Excuse: 'I just don't have the time.' Rubbish! There are 168 hours in a week. Take off nine hours a night for sleep, that leaves 105 hours a week. Subtract 10 hours a day for work (and let's assume you work six days a week and not five), that's 60 hours, that leaves 45 hours of spare time. You could fit another working week in that time, and many people do!

For most people, it's not lack of time, it's lack of direction.

Here is a good, positive exercise for you:

Write a list of your strong points, eg. drive, desire, enthusiasm, ambition, attitudes, your skills, whether you are teachable, open-minded, prepared to learn, and so on.

1..

2..

3..

4..

5..

6..

7..

8..

9..

10...

As you can see, you do have strengths. Most of your self-limiting beliefs are, guess what, nonsense!

Many people who are successful and achieve outstanding results only have a few major strengths, but they learn how to make the most of them.

Look again at the strengths that you have.

The entire Impact System™ is about getting favourable results in your life. Those favourable results come from strengths that are deep inside you. That is where they come from and they have always been there.

Look positively at your results and don't beat yourself up. Remember; 'practice makes progress', not perfect.

Think positively, and each time you take an action step in a directed way, you become better.

Empathy

This is a skill that took me a long time to understand.

You must have heard people say, "Try to see my point of view," or "Put yourself in my shoes".

It gets a bit frustrating when people can't see things from your perspective, or understand a specific problem or challenge you may be going through. I can honestly say that when this has happened to me, I have felt let down, a tad disappointed. I've lost a little trust with the person who couldn't, or wouldn't, understand my point of view.

And I'm sure that other people have been unhappy with me when I haven't listened to them.

Georgia, my wife, is a master of listening, creating trust and empathy. She genuinely listens to what the other person is saying. And even if she disagrees with that other person's point of view, she gives them 100% of her attention and doesn't interrupt them when they speak.

Georgia subscribes to the view that everyone is entitled to their opinion, whatever their opinion is. When she listens to them speaking, she makes mental notes of any key points she might disagree with, and that she might want to question after the other person has finished. She tries to put herself in their situation and to relate to their feelings about what is being discussed. Then she asks questions.

For example, if the person is presenting an idea, she won't say, "That idea would never work." She will say something like, "How do you see this idea working?" As you can see, the question is not only a positive approach, but a subtle way of creating trust and empathy. It shows that you are interested in their point of view.

Georgia's favourite self-development book is by Dale Carnegie, *How to Win Friends and Influence People*. It's well worth a read. In it, he says:

> You can make more friends in one month by being genuinely interested in them than you can make in one year by trying to get others interested in you.

Self-knowledge

Some years ago, I had the good fortune to go on a Telecom Plus cruise around the Mediterranean.

We took in several cities but my favourite was historic Rome. As we toured the city, our guide pointed out an ancient temple of learning. She translated the sign outside. It said simply, 'Know yourself'.

Our guide suggested that the key to Rome's success was personal development and individual mental strength. The key to success, she said, was self-knowledge.

That's why we bang the drum about self knowledge; or self-development. I guess the Romans knew, thousands of years ago, where success starts; internally!

Jim Rohn, in his book *Twelve Pillars*, said 'work harder on yourself than you do on your job.' Your future success will reflect your personal growth. The more you grow the more you can grow your business. Personal growth comes before income growth.

Knowledge

Knowledge is a key factor in any formula for success; but knowledge by itself is rarely effective. There are many people who have a great deal of knowledge but are never successful.

So if knowledge by itself isn't enough, what are the other components? The most important one is application. The key to success is being able to apply your knowledge:

Knowledge x Action = Results

Self-knowledge

Success starts from within yourself. Sometimes, that's the hardest place to look! Start looking in the mirror.

How badly do you want something? What price are you prepared to pay?

The general rule is, whatever the price is for that thing you want, be ready to pay it. You are going to have to, sooner or later.

If you want to improve your golf handicap, lose weight, get a promotion, increase your income, become a better public speaker, you must ask yourself, 'How badly do you want it?'.

I talk about belief in this book. Many other self-development books talk about belief. If you believe you can or you believe you can't, guess what? You're right.

What you believe to be true and what you believe to be possible will eventually become true and possible, but you also need to identify and pay the price.

Look at what you want from this business; prosperity, freedom, success, happiness, abundance? Identify the benefits, and then be prepared to pay the price.

What is the price? Good, old-fashioned, hard work.

I have spoken to many successful people in this business, and they have all said that the price of success was a lot lower than they expected it would be, and that the results more than adequately made up for any price they paid to get there.

Many people do not even dare to dream about being successful because of the fear of having to pay a price.

"All our dreams can come true if we have the courage to pursue them." Walt Disney.

Self-discipline

Don't be confused about time.

Over the years, I have paid hundreds of pounds to go on Time Management courses. Let me save you some money: don't bother. There is no such thing as time management; it's a myth. You can't manage time. Just look at your watch right now. Time happens, whether you want it to or not. You can't make it go faster or slower, it just ticks, ticks, ticks... time keeps going.

All you can do is manage yourself. It's not time management you're looking for, it's self-management.

The most successful Distributors in this business are people who can manage themselves, people who can discipline themselves each and every day to be involved in business-building activities. Those people make the big money.

At the end of each day, 'cash up'. What have you done today to move your business forward or put income into your account?

Remember, though; being productive and being busy are not necessarily the same thing. Just doing things won't create success; you need to be doing the right things.

If you are already working hard at some other occupation when you start this business, it may be a bit of a struggle to invest yet more time in another activity. But think of this as an investment. When you invest money in a business venture, you expect a good return on your investment.

You already know there is very little financial investment required in our business to get you started, but what you do have to invest is - time.

Don't waste your time watching lots of TV, for example; use that time for more productive endeavours.

Time invested NOW will repay you later at an exceptional rate of interest that will free up your time in return!

Perseverance and determination

"I do not think there is any other quality so essential to success of any kind as the quality of perseverance. It overcomes almost everything - even nature."- John D. Rockefeller

It takes time to achieve genuine success. Nothing can take the place of perseverance.

I believe with a passion that those who have a genuine desire to excel will always find a way around or through any problems or challenges that may arise.

Perseverance, persistence and determination will see you through when the fog is thickest, when it seems you shouldn't go on or keep trying. Courage is what you need when your enthusiasm or motivation are low.

Perseverance and determination are key to success in any business, but especially true in Network Marketing. Pay attention to this. Develop rapport with other leaders in the business and you will be a superstar in the Utility Warehouse. Ignore it and you will find yourself down the pub next week with the herd.

While building your business you will suffer all sorts of setbacks, disappointments and frustrations. These are mainly with people. People who promise to come to a meeting won't turn up. People who pretend that they are really interested in starting a business with you will be out when you go round to their house. People you thought would blaze a trail will quit in a short time.

I have met many people who have got to a stage where they thought it wasn't going to work. But they kept going, and it has. It has to! It is impossible not to get where you want to go if you keep speaking to people about the benefits of the services, or the business opportunity.

Every major achievement in the world is built on perseverance.

It doesn't matter how fast you go forward, as long as you are advancing. Every disappointment, rejection, failure or setback, is nothing more than a teacher in disguise. Once you understand this, you can be a star in this business. Don't walk away from rejection or frustration; make it an achievement to conquer them.

Failure is a guaranteed ingredient of success. I have met some seriously successful business people over the last few years. They are in that position because they made more mistakes than other people, heard more no's and had more than their fair share of disappointments, setbacks and heartaches. But they persevered.

You will hear me say this at big events; don't quit. Don't you dare quit. Winners never quit and quitters never win. It's an old cliché, but it's true.

Winston Churchill said this very thing numerous times. In his second term in office, he addressed a graduation ceremony, looked everybody in the face from the podium and delivered one of the shortest but most effective speeches in history:

"Never... give up."

Twenty seconds of silence elapsed while the audience absorbed his words. He continued,

"Never... give up."

Once again, you could have heard a pin drop in the auditorium. There was total silence as the great World War II leader paused for another thirty seconds, and then spoke his final sentence,

"Never... NEVER... give up."

Influence

Never underestimate the power of association.

Your behaviour will be mostly influenced by ideas. Ideas are mostly influenced by education and education is mostly influenced by the people we associate with.

Influence is powerful and influence is subtle. Influence is powerful because it's so subtle.

The influence of those you spend time with is going to have a profound effect on your success or failure. You've heard the phrase, 'peer pressure'. Peer pressure is simply the people that you associate with, applying their influence to move you toward their way of thinking.

Here's what happens. If you associate with people who spend more than they make, the chances are excellent that you will spend more than you make. If you associate with people who go to the pub five nights a week, the chances are excellent that you'll be there too. If you hang around people who don't read many books, the chances are excellent that you won't either. If the people around you are negative and pessimistic, the chances are excellent that you'll become negative and pessimistic too.

We're not usually going to let someone yank us off course and wreck our lives completely, but we do let them nudge us off course. We let them suggest us off course. We let them bump us off course a little at a time, until finally, ten years later, we find ourselves asking, "How did I get here?"

It's not weakness if this happens. But it is weakness to know it's happening and not do anything about it.

There are three, all-important, questions you need to ask yourself. And you need to tell the truth. Let the days of kidding yourself be over. Don't think that it doesn't matter if you kid yourself. Everything matters.

So be honest.

Questions to ask yourself:

1. Who do I allow to influence me?

2. What effect does this have?

> What do they have me listening to?
>
> What do they have me reading?
>
> What do they have me thinking?
>
> How do they have me feeling?
>
> What do they have me saying?
>
> What do they have me settling for?

And most importantly: What does this have me becoming?

3. IS THAT OK?

Of course, I don't know your answers to these questions, but you need to ask them and you need to answer them truthfully.

After studying some of the most successful people in the world, Napoleon Hill said, in his book *Think and Grow Rich*, that the number one reason people fail in life is because they listen to their friends, family and neighbours.

Based on your own answers to the three questions above, here are some actions you can take to correct or improve your association.

1. Disassociation

This is the one that shouldn't be taken lightly, but sometimes you need to consider it. Some people keep associating with people they know are bad for them because they don't want to hurt their feelings.

The sad thing about that is, they are literally sacrificing their life because they are afraid of conflict.

Disassociation doesn't need to mean confrontation. Sometimes you can simply ease yourself out of the wrong person's life.

Just be sure when you do this that it's a conscious effort on your part, or you may end up not accomplishing it.

Disassociation is not an easy action to take, but sometimes it's the most important one.

2. Limiting influence.

You may not want to disassociate completely with some of the people in your life, but it's important that you evaluate how much time you spend with them. It's important to evaluate how much time you spend with that electronic income reducer sitting in the corner of your lounge.

As Jim Rohn suggests, "It's OK to have casual friends, as long as you give them casual time, not serious time. It's OK to spend two hours with some people, but not two days. It's OK to spend two minutes with some people, but not two hours."

Here's how to have an average, mediocre life; spend most of your time on minor things.

Here's how to have a successful life; spend major time with positive influence and minor time with negative influence.

I am not saying that you shouldn't care or have compassion for people you feel are not good for you. You might even be a positive influence in their lives.

I'm just saying that you have to be very careful of the incredible power of influence. Don't be naïve and think it won't have an effect on you.

You must decide what matters to you the most.

3. Good influence

Here's the most positive of the three!

Good influence means spending more time with the right people; men and women of substance. People who understand philosophy and discipline. People of accomplishment and character.

Ask yourself, "Who could I get close to and spend some time with, that will help me progress?"

I have a phrase that describes the people I spend time with; people who 'think right'.

But if you can't find someone right away, you can always start with CDs, books or seminars to give you some daily positive influence, and then you'll start attracting some people who 'think right' too.

But that's one of the greatest aspects of our business; how easy it is to associate with the right people. And this is what the Company training is all about. Until you start to attract the right people, we'll try to give you as much positive influence as we possibly can.

This is called 'association on purpose'. Picking out situations and people where you know associating with them will help you to progress.

New Distributors (and the not-so-new as well!)

Although it is always incredibly important, association has the greatest effect on your business when you're first starting out. You need to be very aware of the effect the people around you are having on your business in the early stages.

While you're starting out, it's best to limit your association with people who don't share your feelings about your ability, and your feelings about this business.

You don't need people to discourage you right now – you need encouragement and support.

And there are a lot of negative opinions about Network Marketing out there – you've got better things to do than listen to them.

More than anything else, try to expand your positive associations as much as possible.

That's why the Career Opportunity Presentations (or 'COPs') that the Company arranges, College of Excellence training and events are so important. Attend as many as you can.

And start feeding your mind by reading books and listening to CDs. By reading 15 pages of a good book a day and listening to a training CD a day, you will increase your knowledge and increase your chances of success.

To summarise: Don't join an easy crowd.

Most of the time, we rise only to the expectations of those around us. If those expectations are low, that's probably as far as you will stretch.

Make sure your expectations are high!

Leadership

Vince Lombardi in his book *What it Takes to be Number One* says,

"Leaders are made, not born. They are made by hard effort, which is the price which all of us must pay to achieve any goal that is worthwhile."

Have the courage to lead. Leaders are solutions-oriented people. Leaders are unselfish givers, not takers.

Negative complainers never achieve great results; they **damage the belief** of people around them and are no fun to work with.

Problem-solving is one of the number one skills that a true leader should possess. You can look through history and identify the greatness of the leader by the scale of the problems they were able to solve. I have had the good fortune to be around some seriously successful people. The thing they do differently from other people is solve bigger problems. It seems the bigger the problem they solve, the bigger the income they earn.

Simple formula:

>   Problem solving = Maturity

>   Maturity = Personal Growth

>   Personal Growth = Taking Action

And I have found:

>   Problem Solving = Income.

So when faced with a problem, don't bury your head in the sand and hope the problem goes away; see how many problems you can solve. If you do that, you will become a better problem-solver. Being a poor problem-solver will result in you being a poor income earner.

Think about babies, and how they deal with problems. They can be hungry, tired and sleepy; they might need to be changed or they might have wind. If a baby has one of those problems, how do they try to rectify it? They cry and whinge. That's how they try to solve their problems, because that's all they know how to do.

Now think about adults, and how they deal with problems. If they are a poor problem-solver, what do they do? Yes, you've guessed it, they cry and whinge! They don't try to solve the problem; they try to lay blame on someone else. But adults should know better.

If you cry and whinge, understand that for your income to go up massively, your problem-solving ability has to be cultivated and improve.

Become a good problem-solver. Become a person people can turn to in times of crisis. Remember that most problems you will be dealing with have little to do with rules or regulations; they are mostly personality problems, people crying and whinging and laying the blame on someone else.

How to solve your own problems

The problems that are the most difficult to solve are the ones where you are personally, emotionally, involved. When you are emotionally involved it is tricky to make the right decision.

Ask yourself these questions:

1. What can I do? Honestly evaluate your options; some solutions require eating a little humble pie. If that is the right step, be mature enough to admit that, and do it.

2. What can I read? I can guarantee that no matter what problem you are facing, someone has written about how to solve it.

3. Who can I ask? If you have done all you can and you have read all you can read, then the third step is: 'Who can I ask?' If you ask first, you will never become a skilled problem-solver, you will always be dependent on someone else.

How to solve other people's problems

Three questions to ask:

1. What can you do about yesterday? The obvious answer is: nothing.

2. Are you there to be part of the problem or part of the solution? That should determine your attitude towards them solving it. Their answer should be, 'To be part of the solution.'

3. Do you understand there is no perfect solution to anything? Hopefully, they will agree.

When you've asked those three questions, proceed with dealing with the problem:

1. Gather the facts. You will know when you have gathered enough facts, when the picture starts to repeat itself from both sides. There are two sides to every story.

2. Understand spotlighting. That is when someone does not want you to notice their faults, so they quickly put the spotlight on the other person to expose theirs. In a personality situation, here is a good rule of thumb; whoever raises the problem first is usually the person at fault and most situations are personality-related.

3. Brainstorm for possible solutions. Ask yourself, "Would this solution work the same every time in the same circumstances?" If it wouldn't, you are probably emotionally involved and you should ask someone else's opinion.

4. Model yourself on someone you respect as a good problem-solver/leader. Ask yourself: "How would they handle this?"

5. Choose the best solution quickly, act upon the solution you choose, make your decision and don't look back. Understand that you are not going to make the correct decision every time. If you make what turns out to be a poor decision, learn from it so you can make a better one next time. Move on.

None of us can avoid the storms of life. To be a Leader, and to be in for the long run will require you, from time to time, to stand against the opinions of the crowd. You may have to swim against the current and stand up for what you believe in.

You will need to work harder and smarter.

You will need to invest your time into those things that will help you build a strong and secure future. You will have set-backs, but you will be strong enough to get up again. You will have learnt from your mistakes and will have improved your business based on action, experience and acquired wisdom.

You can do all of this.

Motivation

If you're going to make this work, if you want this business to give you the opportunity to make big changes in your life, if you want to keep going when times get tough (because they will), then focus on these five key elements that will fire your motivation:

1. Burning Desire

You have to want it. You have to develop your desire. Desire comes from deep within you, but desire can be cultivated. It can be cultivated through the Impact System™. It can be cultivated by getting involved with the right group of people. It can be cultivated by having clear goals. It can be cultivated in many ways.

Cultivate your desire.

2. Making the decision to pay the price

You have to know what you want. Many people I meet can tell me what they don't want. Most people spend more time planning their two-week holiday every year than they do planning their future.

Decide what you want.

3. Taking action

Decision turns you in a new direction; action takes you towards that new direction. Here is a great word that goes with action: massive. Take massive action. Don't be like the

Distributor who says, "I will just hand out a few brochures and see how it goes." They will always be broke. Don't be like the one who says, "I will try a home meeting and see what happens." You can guess their bank account. If you are going to take action, make sure it is all-out massive action. That is where real success comes from.

Take massive action.

4. Feeling sick and tired

Sick and tired means you don't like your life as it is. You have had it up to here. You're not putting up with it any more. It's the point where you say to yourself, "I am sick and tired of being sick and tired. I want change!"

You can live your life one way for years and years. But then one day you draw a line in the sand. You say, "I'm sick and tired of this." That can be the day your life changes forever.

Don't put up with sick and tired.

5. Tenacity

Tenacity means, "I will do whatever it takes." Tenacity means, "You can count on me. I will be there."

People will tell you the grass is greener, but let me tell you , it is just as difficult to cut!

You pick your mountain in life and wherever that mountain is, you say, "I am going to the top." There will be some people who will tell you, "You can't climb mountains, you don't have the experience." You say, "I am going to the top." Somebody else may say, "Choose another mountain, that one's too steep and rocky." You say, "I am going to the top." Someone else may say, "Come on, not that one. That's too slippery. Climb this other, easier one." You say, "I'm going to the top."

Somebody else may simply say it can't be done. You say, "Listen, I am going to the top. You're either going to see me waving from the top or collapsed on the side. —I'm not coming back."

Remember the times in your life when you took a casual approach or had a weak attitude? I bet you didn't accomplish what you set out to accomplish.

When you are climbing your mountain you have got to have a do or die attitude. That's called major tenacity. It is also the difference between success and failure.

There is something about a stubborn, do or die attitude; it works. Nothing can stand in your way.

Have a do or die attitude.

Producing fruit

"If a tree is given minimal nourishment, it will survive but have slow growth. If nourishment is given over what is needed for life, the tree will grow in all directions; but if a tree is given nourishment over and beyond what is needed to support life, needed for growth and more, it will produce fruit - fruit is the overflow, surplus of excess nourishment."

John Grapey

We, as individuals, are like this. And in Network Marketing, our businesses are a reflection of us; if you want your business to grow and bear fruit, you must grow and bear fruit yourself.

And what is your nourishment?

Books and CDs

If you do not read, you must change. Start reading.

If you do not listen, you must change. Start listening.

Start learning.

For your life to change, the change must start with you.

You're reading this book. That's a good start!

PART 2

GETTING
STARTED RIGHT

Building a team – leveraging time

Building a team is the basic principle of Network Marketing, what it's all about.

It's how you create a big business, from small amounts of regular work of your own.

	Team members at start of month	Each team member introduces one person	You introduce one person	Total team members at end of month
Jan	-	-	1	1
Feb	1	+ 1	+ 1	= 3
Mar	3	+ 3	+ 1	= 7
Apr	7	+ 7	+ 1	= 15
May	15	+ 15	+ 1	= 31
June	31	+ 31	+ 1	= 63
July	63	+ 63	+ 1	= 127
August	127	+ 127	+ 1	= 255
Sept	255	+ 255	+ 1	= 511
Oct	511	+ 511	+ 1	= 1,023
Nov	1,023	+ 1,023	+ 1	= 2,047
Dec	2,047	+ 2,047	+ 1	= 4,095

Look at what happens if you introduce just one person a month, and teach all of those individuals to do the same. Just imagine what will happen when each get a few customers!

So, by introducing – or sponsoring – just 12 people and teaching them to do the same, your group has grown to over 4,000 in just one year!

It doesn't always work like this, of course. But if your team grows to only a quarter of the amount in this example, 25% of 4,095 is still a group of around 1,000 people.

John Paul Getty said, "I would much rather have 1% of a hundred people's efforts, than 100% of my own." Wise words!

1,000 people x one hour worked each = 1,000 hours per week. That's a good business.

In our business you can work smart as well as hard, by introducing like-minded people who see the value of leveraging their time and building a team.

When you first join our business, your business is you. If you want to build a big business you must find five - seven serious people to sponsor. You will need to sponsor and recruit more than five to find five who want to take this business as seriously as you.

As time wins out, you will find good people and help them start building their own teams.

It takes time. In your early days in the business you will be exchanging 90% of your time for 10% return on investment, just like a traditional business. But as your business begins to develop over a three to five year time period - you will be investing 10% of your time for 90% of your income, giving you huge time and money freedom.

TIME vs MONEY

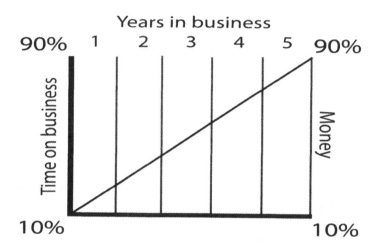

Do not confuse 'time *in* the business' with 'time *on* the business'. It is only 'activity based time' that counts

Five simple steps to building your team,

1. Talk to a friend about making extra money.

2. Tell them about our vehicle- the Company and services, the back-up and support.

3. Help them understand the power of leveraging time and how the money works.

4. Look for commitment.

5. Have your new Distributors repeat these simple steps.

Circle of success

So let's see how you do it.

First steps for the new Distributor

1. Become your own first customer

The Impact System™ assumes that you have signed up for all the basic services that the Utility Warehouse provides.

If you want to earn a substantial residual income in this business, please don't be naive and think you don't need to use the services yourself.

You can't be a Mercedes dealer and turn up to work in a BMW! It wouldn't instil confidence and belief in the customers.

But there's more to it. It's very important you obtain all the services that the Company provides for your own use, for many reasons:

- **For your personal benefit.** You'll save money!

- **Develops knowledge.** You'll understand how the products and services work.

- **Increases belief in the services.** You'll understand how good the Company is at what it does.

- **As you use all of the services, you will develop the belief and conviction necessary to share them effectively.** People buy because of how you feel about the benefits of the services, not because of how much you know about them.

So, sign up for the services. You'll also find that your best sales tool will be your Utility Warehouse bill.

2. Make time

The next step is to make a specific time commitment to building your business. Then use that time for productive activity.

The Impact System™ is designed to support long-term, sustained commitment.

This is not a lottery. It's not a game of chance. To build a successful business takes time and effort.

Consistency and persistence will be the biggest determining factors in your long-term success.

3. Start to educate yourself

First off:
- Watch the *What's it all about?* DVD.
- Watch it again.
- Listen to *Building your Network Marketing Business* by Jim Rohn.

Read, listen to and watch everything you can get your hands on that will positively impact the way you function in this business.

Read the Company Compensation Plan and highlight it; you can avoid all kinds of future mistakes if you understand the rules at the start.

Become fully informed about how our business works.

4. Lead by example

Your future team will do what you did when you got started. Start leading by example now.

Set up a time within 48 hours to meet with your sponsor/upline.

Do not take this meeting lightly! I believe it is imperative that you meet with your sponsor/upline in the first 48 hours, either face to face, over the phone or in a group setting. The Company calls this Meeting 1, and provides you with forms to help you do the meeting.

This is how the meeting works. Remember, it's for you this time, but it's for your team members in future.

Six key questions for new Distributors

a: Do you want to build a big business or a small business?

b: In the short term how much money do you want to earn from this?

c: What is your WHY, your key reason to make this work?

d: Have you signed up for all the services? -To be successful you need to use the services yourself or you will fail.

e: Have you started your contact list? It is a free and very valuable resource.

f: Do you know how to invite?

5. Listen to *Making the Shift* by Darren Hardy during your second day

6. Complete your list. You will have spoken about this when you met your sponsor/upline. Take the time in the first few days to complete your contact list.

7. Listen to *Making the Shift* by Darren Hardy and *Building Your Network Marketing Business* by Jim Rohn during your third day.

8. Start your training. Log on to the Extranet and do the online training. Do it again. Do it as much as you need to make sure you understand what the Company does.

9. Get three-way calling. Three-way calling is a very effective tool, especially if you want your sponsor/upline's help in recruiting a group. It's a minimal cost, and well worth it. Call Customer Service to get it.

10. Get a diary, and use it. It's so important to make sure you schedule a Career Opportunity Presentation (COP) every fortnight.

11. Get a diary, and use it. It's so important to make sure you schedule your College of Excellence Training.

12. Get a diary, and use it. It's so important to make sure you schedule upcoming special events.

13. Identify your upline. If you don't know who they are – call Partner Services and find out!

14. Get your questions answered. Be sure to have any concerns or questions answered at this time. Ask your upline, or Partner Services.

15. Keep a tight rein on your new team members! They may be full of enthusiasm, but tell them not to say anything to anyone about the services or the opportunity until you have gone through some basic scripts with them. If they go off before they're ready, they will not succeed, which means they will get disheartened, and they will stop.

16. Make sure all your new team members have an answer service. You're going to want to be able to leave them messages!

17. Make sure your new team members do numbers 1 –16.

Prepare to take action

When you take action, the first thing you need to do is think.

I take great comfort in thinking about those who have gone before and built a large team. They've mastered the '10-ton telephone' (it feels that hard to pick up!) and they've become successful.

I suppose that's why we all need mentors. We all need to have somebody putting positive input into our life, even if it is just to give us a push along.

My goal is to get you to pick up the phone and make the call. If I can help you do that, I have served you well.

I am constantly thinking about how I can creatively communicate truths that have been written about before by many people in Network Marketing. But my aim is simple enough. When I share what I have learned with you, I am trying to open up your mind, so that you can begin to think and take action.

Here are some of the questions I ask myself:

Why is it that two people can sit in the same seminar and hear the same words, yet one will leave that seminar and achieve great success while the other will continue in their mediocrity?

Why is that?

Why is it that someone with little or no formal education can still attain great wealth, while educated people can end up with nothing?

Why is that?

Why is it that people with small talent and great resolve achieve so much, while others with great talent and no resolve achieve so little?

Why is that?

And - what separates a winner from a loser?

Here are a few questions for you to ask yourself:

"What will happen if I don't make that telephone call?"

"What might happen if I do make that telephone call?"

"Where will I be in five years if I do what they have shown me to do?"

"Where will I be in five years if I put my feet up and don't follow the basic instructions in this little book, which is designed to help me get to where I want to be in five years?"

Questions are powerful simply because they encourage you to think. If we don't question ourselves, we simply float down the river like everybody else.

Questioning pushes us out of our comfort zone and into the area where we are required to take action.

Why is that?

Here's a question that has spurred me on:

"What will happen if I take this action, and what will happen if I don't do it?"

It is the kind of question that makes you feel uncomfortable. It causes you to take a serious look at your life. It makes you take stock of where you are, what you're doing and where you're going.

Questions that cause us to think about our life will prepare us to take the next successful step.

They will prepare us to take action.

Contacting and inviting

If you are successful in getting people to look at the business, you will be successful in building a team. The bottom line is that much of your success will result from inviting people in the right way

Be proud

Be proud of your business opportunity. Never be shy about prospecting or sharing this great business idea. If you are, it means you are not proud of what you have to offer.

You should be so excited that you are telling everybody about this. If people understood properly what the top Distributors know, everyone would want to take this business seriously!

There are ordinary people who join this business having never done anything like this before, and go on to build huge teams, drive new free cars, go on free holidays, get thousands of pounds worth of free Share Options and earn thousands a month! They are happy, fulfilled people.

And the price for enjoying this lifestyle? Those who choose to recruit have to admit – proudly - that Network Marketing is part of their career. Does that sound so hard?

Who to invite

With a bit of work, you should be able to make a list of over 100 people you know by name.

Give everyone you know and meet the opportunity to see this business and make their own decision. It is not your responsibility to make everyone see this business as you do, or to try and convince people that it's the business for them.

Your only responsibility is to share it with everyone and let them make their own decision.

Don't prejudge someone based on your assumptions – you have no idea really who may or may not want to take up this opportunity. Have an open mind. You may well be surprised.

How to invite

There are lots of ways you can contact and invite people. You may choose to explore different methods as you grow your business. But to start with, focus on contacting and inviting people by phone. This way, you will develop vital communication skills that will serve you well at the start of your business, and that you will be able to build on later as well.

The purpose of the 'inviting' phone call is to set up an appointment for your prospect – someone you think will be interested in the business – to look at the business. Your goal should be to create curiosity and excitement. Answer as few questions as possible and get a firm commitment from them to look at the business.

It's important for you to understand one vital point, and make sure your new Distributors understand it too: never try to explain this business over the phone.

We have tools that can help you explain our business opportunity, but they work best when you're face-to-face with someone.

Over the phone, it's really easy to give the wrong impression of what this business is about.

I was approached by several people about Telecom Plus in the early days. Over the phone, they gave me the impression that this was a telephone sales door-knocking job... and guess what, I didn't listen to them!

It's important to get in front of someone to show them the business.

Different approaches

One important point to remember is: you are not the issue!

You are the messenger, not the message. Please do not think you need to be successful first before you share the business opportunity with someone. Your objective is to share the information, and sell them on how good the business is, not on how good you are.

Commit to the process of becoming a good inviter.

Understand that the best you can do today is not the best you will do in the future; it's just the best you can do today.

You will learn something new from every contact you make.

Another key to remember is never to apologise during the invite. You are coming from a point of strength here; our business is not on trial or test.

There are basically three different approaches you can use (and teach!) for contacting prospects:

- the direct approach
- the indirect approach, and

- the 'Who do you know?' approach.

The direct approach

Use this approach with people you know well; people you feel have a good level of respect or friendly feelings toward you.

If you are new to the business, I would suggest the conversation should last no more than a few minutes and you should always start the call with, "It's just a quick call because I am running late for," eg. an appointment or picking up the children, so you can get off the phone once you've made the appointment and not get dragged into trying to explain the business over the phone.

Example:

"Hi John. It's Stephan. How are you? [etc] It's just a quick call as I'm on my way out. May I ask you, is the time right for you to look at other ways of making money? Are you open to looking at business opportunities?"

The answer will be "Yes", "No" or "What's it about?"

Tell them you would like to explain it over the phone but it will take too long and besides, you're running late as it is... it will be far easier to show them because you have something they need to see.

Tell them you're free tomorrow or the next day. Does that fit in with them?

Here is another example:

"Hi Mary. It's Stephan. How are you? [etc] It's a quick call as I'm just on my way out... Look, if I could show you a way to set up an additional income stream without interfering with your job or business, could you find thirty minutes in the next couple of days to look at it?"

Here is another example:

This is good for anyone you know who is dissatisfied in any area of their life. It could be that they hate their job/boss, they're afraid of redundancy, would like more holidays, to upgrade the car, pay for something special for a loved one, etc... but they can't afford it.

"Hi John. It's Stephan. How are you? [etc] It's just a quick call because I am on my way out to an appointment at the bank. Can I ask you something? A while ago you said you hated your job and would like out. Were you serious or joking?" [John says he is serious] *"I can't go into it now but I might have a way out for you. Can we get together for thirty minutes tomorrow or the next day so I can run an idea by you?"*

Or it could just be as simple as:

"Mary, I'm glad I got hold of you! Listen, I only have a minute. I'm just running out of the door, but I have something I need to talk to you about. How soon could we get together?"

Example: approaching existing customers to become Distributors

"Hi John/Mary...it's just a quick call. I know you have been a customer for a while now, well the UWDC are looking for satisfied customers to become distributors and there is a

Business opportunity presentation on Monday evening at the
..... I would appreciate it if you could come along to find out
about it and how it could benefit you."

The indirect approach

You should use this approach when you are contacting
someone who might be perceived to be better or more
successful than you; in other words, when you are 'recruiting
up'.

The perception has nothing to do with the reality.

'Recruiting up' does not mean they actually are better than
you or me; it simply means they may have a bigger circle of
influence or a better contact base than you. The basic
philosophy of this approach is to play yourself down, and play
up to their ego, their sense of their own importance.

Example:

"Hello Mr. Smith. How are you? It's Stephan Longworth here.
It's just a very quick call. I have always had a lot of respect for
you in business. I am getting involved in an opportunity that
has some really exciting potential and I would really value your
professional opinion on it. Could we get together for twenty
minutes tomorrow or [another day] so I can run an idea by
you?"

Example:

"Hello Mary. It's Stephan Longworth. How are you? It's just a
quick call. I've always had a lot of respect for you and the
success you have had in business. May I ask you - do you keep

your income options open?" ["Yes"] "Great. I can't go into it now, as I am late for an appointment, but can we get together tomorrow or [another day] for 20 minutes? I want to run an idea by you."

The 'Who do you know?' approach

You should use this approach for people who are very successful, or if you don't know if they are 'dissatisfied'.

It's basically, "Who do you know who would like to make more money?"

It gives them the chance to say, "What about me?" if they are interested. Or they may give some names of people they know if the timing is not right for them.

Example:

"John, it's Stephan. Just a quick call. I have joined a very exciting company, listed on the London stock market, and we are looking for some sharp people who might be interested in setting up a lucrative additional income stream without affecting their job/business. Who do you know that would fit that description?"

Example:

"Mary, it's Stephan. Just a quick call, as I am on my way out. You have been on my mind to call. Can I ask you - who do you know that is entrepreneurial and would like to make some serious money part-time? We are expanding in your area."

Example:

If you are talking to someone you've just met, the normal questions come up, "Where are you from?" and, "What do you do?"

Here's how to use this approach.

"Where about are you from?" [They answer] "Really? The company I do business with is looking at expanding in that area! May I ask - who do you know that I could give some information to that would like to make more money?" ["Me!"]

Re-contacting people you have told about the business

There are countless examples of people who have joined our business 12-36 months after they were first approached.

If people on your list do not join, you must re-contact them every three months. Their circumstances might have changed.

Example:

"Mary, hi, it's Stephan. It's just a quick call to touch base with you. Do you remember a while ago I showed you/spoke to you about our business? I must apologise because I didn't do it justice or show you the bigger picture. I have been involved for a while now and it's going really well. Would it be OK if I sent you the latest information, so you can evaluate it properly for yourself? I understand the timing might not be right for you, but you might know someone who would be interested. Thanks."

You have nothing to lose by doing this – and everything to gain, as does your prospect!

Leveraging a new team member from your list

This technique can turn one new distributor into several new team members, creating excitement and momentum in your team

Example:

"Hi John, it's Stephan. Are you ok to talk, it's just a quick call? The reason for my call is that you recently looked at the Utility Warehouse business opportunity and said that it would benefit you and your families future, however you were a bit busy and were thinking about starting it in a couple of months, is that still the case John?

OK, well I've called you as I've just helped someone get started with us and they are going to do really well and I wondered if it would benefit you and your family if I could put this person in your business to give you a flying start. I didn't want you to miss out so I called you first! Would that benefit you? Great, ok in that case you need to register today so I can do this for you."

This same approach can be used to build your existing team

Example:

"Hi Mary, its Stephan. Are you ok to talk? Mary I would love to help you get to Team Leader (next level) in your business and I have a new person just joined who I think will do really well and I would love to put him in your team. Now I can do this in the next seven days if you are able to bring in a new Distributor yourself in this time frame, would that benefit you?"

Answering questions, overcoming objections

The majority of people that you contact will have some questions or objections. These will usually be out of curiosity, if you have done your job correctly. So with that in mind, it is important to be prepared for the questions and objections that will come up.

Let's look at the most common ones:

1. What they said: "What is it?" or "Tell me more!"

What they meant: "What is it?" or "Tell me more!"

This is only natural. Here are a few responses to that question:

"John, I would if I could but as I said, I am running a bit late. And what I need to share with you is 90% visual."

"Mary, it's like a haircut; you need to be there to fully understand what I'm talking about."

"John, I can appreciate your question and I don't want to sound evasive over the phone. All I can tell you is this is a massive opportunity with a PLC business with lots of high-street names joining. If I could effectively explain it over the phone I would, but I need to show you how it works."

"Mary, if I could, I would, but I am too new in the business to explain it to you effectively over the phone. I need to show you."

And get a commitment...

"That is why we need to get together asap. Is tomorrow good for you or would the next day be better?"

2. What they said: "I don't have the time."

What they meant: "You haven't shown me enough value to justify my time."

Responses:

"John, I wouldn't ask you to give up any of your time if I didn't think it would be worth your while."

"I fully understand and appreciate how valuable your time is. But if I could show you a way to create a second revenue stream using my time and your contacts; would you be willing to spend 30 minutes with me to get the facts?"

"Mary, I am only asking for 30 minutes. If I am wrong, you've lost half an hour. But what if I'm right?"

"John, when I thought of who I would like to work with and who could benefit most from this business, I thought of you. If you can't find 30 minutes to check it out that's OK, but I was just thinking of you."

And get a commitment...

"I can work around your diary; would daytime or evening be better for you?"

3. What they said: "Is this Network Marketing?"

What they meant: "Is this Network Marketing?"

Response:

Ask them what they know about Network Marketing.

If the answer is positive, just say, "Great. What do you know about the industry?"

If the answer is negative, point out that Telecomplus is a PLC, listed on the London Stock Exchange. They have taken the best bits from the industry and discarded the worst bits and they're taking Network Marketing into the 21st century.

And get a commitment...

"When can we get together so I can show you the facts on the company?"

4. What they said: "Is it pyramid selling?"

What they meant: "Is it legal and ethical?"

"No Thanks! Looks like a Pyramid Scheme!"

Responses:

"I am not sure what a pyramid is, can you explain it to me?"
[They usually can't, but will try to give an answer so they don't
look like an idiot] *"This is nothing like that!"* [Point out the
credibility and the fact that the Company is a PLC on the
London Stock Exchange].

*"John, if this was what you think it is, I would not be involved
in it. You really need to look at it and get the information
before you make any judgment! You're absolutely right,
though, it is important for a business to be legal and ethical
and after you have looked at the facts, I hope you will see that
this is, and that will answer your concerns."*

5. What they said: "I need to talk to my partner."

**What they meant: "I need reassurance and support. Can you
help me?"**

Response:

*"I think the best thing to do is for all three of us to sit down
and discuss it together. That way your partner will get all the
information also and then the two of you can make a
decision."*

And get a commitment...

*"Does that make sense? Would you like to get together for
lunch tomorrow or would Sunday be better?"*

6. What they said: "What is the name of the company?"

What they meant: "What is the name of the company?"

Response:

"It's the Utility Warehouse, which is a major company that is operated by Telecom Plus PLC. Have you heard of Telecom Plus? It's incredible what they have been able to accomplish, even in the recession."

And get a commitment...

"When can we get together so I can show you the information and benefits?"

7. What they said: "I'm not interested!"

If they say this, you have said too much! Say less next time.

Give them a recruitment tool – a DVD (*What's it all About?*) or brochure – and ask them at least to review the information before they make a decision.

The feel/felt/found approach

One of the best tools for overcoming objections is the feel/felt/found approach.

You never want to get into an argument over a question or an objection. You want to help them get past it. This approach helps you do that. Here is how it works:

Prospect: "I don't have the time."

*"Mary, I know exactly how you **FEEL**, I **FELT** the same way, but let me tell you what I **FOUND**. You don't need a lot of time to*

get started, in fact, I have only put a few hours per week in to help create a financial safety net for the future and it's great."

Prospect: "I don't have the money."

*"John, I know how you **FEEL**, I **FELT** the same way. I was unsure about finding the money, but this is what I **FOUND**. Once I checked it all out, I felt comfortable with the UWDC because they have a refund policy. I felt comfortable finding the money because there was no risk, for a very big opportunity."*

You get the idea. Try this with any objection; I think you will be pleasantly surprised with the results. You are agreeing with them by saying, "I know how you feel. I felt the same way", and you're giving them the solution by telling them what happened to you.

It is a powerful technique.

Getting a firm commitment

Get a commitment from a prospect as to:

- Location – where to meet
- Time – when to meet
- Date – what day to meet
- Partner – who to meet

And...

- That they will be there!
- That they will do you the courtesy of letting you know if they are unable to make the appointment.

Or get a commitment that they will review any information that you send; a DVD (*What's it all About?*), brochure, etc...

- That they will listen or view it within 24 hours and get back to you.

How do you get a commitment?

Your prospect's two greatest motivations are the fear of loss and the desire for gain.

Fear of loss is when people feel they will miss out if they don't do something. Advertisers bombard us with fear of loss everywhere we turn; half-price furniture sale, one day only... beat the price increase till Tuesday; two for one offer while stocks last... limited offers are given with a deadline and the items for sale are restricted to a definite time frame.

I have found that the best way to get people to review your information or come to a COP or home meeting is the threat of a 'take away'.

Example: "*Mary, watch this DVD tonight, it's only 15 minutes long, but I need it back asap because I have Tom waiting to watch it.*"

What you must convey is, "I would love to have you on board, but I am going to go on with this, with or without you".

It's not an arrogant attitude, it's a point of strength attitude.

No-one wants to be part of your test.

If they think you're just dabbling at this business they won't come to your COP or home meeting.

Don't tell your prospect that there is a COP every fortnight for the next 12 months; if they think they can put it off, they won't attend. You need to inject urgency and fear of loss.

Example: *"John, you said you were interested in our business, what are you doing next Tuesday evening for an hour that can't be put off? We are holding a company overview at the [hotel]. It will give you a clear understanding of the opportunity. I'm not sure when the next one is after that, and I don't want you to miss out."*

The close

Just... get off the phone!

Many new Distributors spend a few minutes making the appointment and because they can't quite believe it happened, they spend the next 10 minutes cancelling it! After you have confirmed their commitment to meet with you, it is important to get off the phone.

Call to confirm

This is so important. Some people are afraid to call their prospect to confirm the appointment, but it is **critical** that you do. I am sure you would prefer to know if they can't make the appointment before you drive across town and waste your valuable time.

When you are calling to confirm the appointment, make sure to start the call by telling your prospect that you're in a hurry, but that they will not be disappointed when you meet. Do not start answering more questions.

Commitment

"Commitment is doing the thing you said you would do, long after the mood in which you said it has passed."

You won't succeed in presenting this business without commitment. Let's look at what that means.

It is absolutely imperative that you believe in what you are promoting. If you don't believe the Utility Warehouse can provide a person with a financial back-up plan or a good part-time business, or if you don't believe in the services the Company provides, then you won't – and shouldn't – try to convince someone else to believe in them.

Start with the end in mind

It is important to know where you are going before you start your presentation. The plan or goal for every presentation is to either sponsor them into the business, get them to try the services or get a referral. Go into the presentation with that in mind.

Without the desire to help someone towards a positive result, you simply will not be successful. You must recognise the importance of 'closing', and have the desire to be able to influence your prospect towards taking a positive action that could well change their life for the better.

Learn to persuade

Do not spend all of your time trying to impress your prospect. Spend your time persuading the prospect to take action and your time will be rewarded.

Be a good listener

To get really good, you must be a good listener. People will constantly be communicating their feelings towards your presentation through how they act and what they say.

A good listener listens to understand where the other person is coming from, and does not have a quick reply.

A good listener understands that it's more important to listen to the prospect than it is to show them how much they know about this business.

So listen more, and talk less.

Have courage

You need to speak to people about the benefits of the business opportunity and services. It might be a little uncomfortable at first, but you have to do it if you want to be successful.

Through sheer repetition, you will gain the confidence necessary to become successful.

You need to have the courage to present the opportunity and to help people make a decision, rather than procrastinate.

Learn to handle rejection

Whatever happens, you will get some no's.

No matter how fantastic your presentation, no matter if you have done everything right, you will still get them (there's a good CD and book about this - *Go for No*). The no's come with the territory and you need to learn how to handle rejection when it occurs.

First, regard every rejection as an opportunity to learn. Review your presentation and approach. You can even ask your prospect if there was anything you might have said or done to make it better; how you could improve next time?

Second, remind yourself that in this business, as in many other businesses, it's a numbers game. You must understand that a certain percentage of people you contact are going to say no.

You can't hope to be perfect every time, but you can improve your effectiveness by improving your presentation. Just keep stepping up to the spot to take the shot and eventually you will hit the goal.

- Colonel Sanders of Kentucky Fried Chicken fame made close to 1,000 calls and spent nights sleeping in his car before he made his first sale.

- Thomas Edison failed many times before he succeeded in changing our world by creating the incandescent light bulb.

- Andrew Lindsay MBE, our Chief Executive, lost plenty of boat races before he won his Olympic Gold medal.

Finally, do not take the no's as a personal rejection. Don't get upset; sometimes you win, sometimes you lose. That's just the way it is.

Be persistent, and persevere

On my way home from leading an advanced training session, I got a message on my phone. It was from a new Distributor on my 11th level, who had been given my number at a 'Getting

Started' training session a week before. He wanted to meet with me.

As you can imagine, I get requests like this all the time. This individual had already sent me several texts and emails, and I was impressed by his persistent 'never give up' attitude. I simply said to him that I was very busy, and I normally meet up with people when they have a few customers and Distributors under their belt.

I told him to contact his upline, who could meet with them to discuss how they could move forward. Or, he could meet me at the COP in Manchester in two hours time.

I didn't expect that he could get organised, changed into business clothes, drop the kids off with someone, and get to the COP in two hours as they lived near Chester, a good 38 miles from the venue, but he texted me back, saying, "see you in two hours".

I was taken aback by his tenacity. We met and I am pleased to tell you that Paul is a Senior Team Leader today, and well on his way to reaching Group Leader in the business.

One of the differences between the 'will be's' from the 'want to be's' is a dogged determination to give it another go. Even in a situation like the one in this example, other people would have given up.

When I made a decision to make this business work, I called 37 people I knew over a two-hour period. I got 13 answer phones, eight no's/not interested, 16 agreed to meet me, 10 turned up and six joined. Three quit and three are still with me today, from over 12 years ago. Those three people have generated a customer base in excess of 39,000.

Don't give up. Just think what it could stop you achieving.

Enthusiasm

Enthusiasm sells. Get enthusiastic about your business in your own way, but get enthusiastic! In a world where everybody is selling something, whether it's a great idea, a service or a product, your best colleague is enthusiasm.

But don't fake enthusiasm. People can spot fake enthusiasm a mile off.

Lack of enthusiasm will bring you down

One of the major reasons why people don't build large teams is lack of enthusiasm; they don't get to events regularly, so they don't see the bigger picture.

People who don't attend events and associate with those who have succeeded in this business, don't get the belief in this opportunity. This means:

1. Their enthusiasm is low when they speak to friends, family members or associates, so they don't communicate that they have a special opportunity to offer.

2. They convey a lack of belief to others so, in turn, their friends, family and associates just pay them lip service as well.

I am not saying you should be jumping on chairs, whooping and saying 'hallelujah'. But you might have heard the phrases, 'people hear the music and not the words', or 'the sizzle sells the steak'?

You need a level of genuine enthusiasm and conviction to cut through the static in people's heads! Enthusiasm wins.

The last four letters of enthus**iasm** stand for:

I

Am

Sold

Myself

One of the main reasons we advise team members to go to events regularly is to keep their enthusiasm and belief levels up. It works!

A few Golden Rules to help build enthusiasm

- Recognise the importance of attending events regularly

- Concentrate on, and picture, all the possible benefits to yourself that this business has to offer

- Commit yourself to the importance of being enthusiastic about the services and the opportunity. **Make sure that you are a customer yourself so that you know how good the services – and savings – are**

- Remind yourself daily that what you are doing is *genuinely* helping others to save £££s or make £££s.

- Focus on the positive, and eliminate the negative

- Remember: if you are not enthusiastic about what you do, nobody else will be! But if you are enthusiastic – others will be too. Enthusiasm is contagious!

- **Look** enthusiastic, **Sound** enthusiastic, **Feel** enthusiastic.

There is a rule in business and in life; people buy people first. And just as importantly; people buy enthusiastic people first.

Different ways to present the business opportunity

There are several different ways to present the benefits of the business opportunity effectively, but whichever method you are using, they all have this in common:

Elements of the presentation:

- Company
- Services
- Support
- Compensation

Goal for each presentation:

- Involve the prospect in the opportunity
- Create a Club member
- Get referrals

Different methods of presenting the business

1. One-on-one

This method should be one of your most successful ways of presenting the opportunity. One of the biggest positives is the fact that most people are happy to meet you in a one-on-one setting, and the more people see the business, you will be more successful!

How to conduct a one-on-one presentation

- Invite your prospect! Go through the procedure described before, in *Contacting and inviting*

- Dress for business

- Have your own bill with you

- Take your presentation folder; an information pack including brochure/DVD/CD

- Be punctual

- Ask questions and show interest in them. Your aim is to find out what is important to your prospects and then use it later in your presentation

- Tell your story. In a brief way, share how you got involved and why you're excited about it

- Share the elements of the business: the Company, credibility, services

- Show them the money: do the Martini presentation

- Discuss, 'What's in it for them?' No one will join just to help you with your dreams and goals

- When you asked your prospect some questions at the beginning of the presentation, you should have gathered some clues as to what was your prospect's 'hot button'; what it is they really want. Show them how they can achieve what they desire by becoming a Utility Warehouse Distributor

- Move towards a positive result; either signing as a Distributor or agreeing to a second exposure at a local

COP. Your prospect should then have had enough information to make an informed decision.

2. The Career Opportunity Presentation (COP), hotel or home meetings

- Invite your prospects!
- Invite three times the number of people you would like to attend
- Call to confirm
- Dress for business
- On your way to the COP, pick up your top prospect
- Be prepared; take application forms! Also, have some information available (recruiting CDs and DVDs). If they don't sign up there and then, don't let your prospects go home empty-handed.

3. Home or hotel meetings

These are probably one of the fastest ways to build your team because you can expose many people at a time to the business opportunity.

Have some pleasant music playing. For home meetings, have some snacks and drinks available. Make sure the room is cool; you don't want the room to be overheated and uncomfortable. Set up enough chairs for about two-thirds of the number of people you expect. Add chairs as more people arrive, if you need to.

Please note: don't invite people with a history of a negative attitude to these presentations.

- Welcome your guests. Avoid talking about the business before the meeting. Ask people about their favourite subject; themselves! If they ask how many people you are expecting, say, "A few". That way they won't know if you have had a low or high turnout

- Never leave the room while the meeting is in progress

- Ask people to turn their phones to silent and hold questions until the end

- Tell your story. In a brief way, share how you got involved and why you're excited about it

- Share the elements of the business: the Company, credibility, services

- Show them the money; do the Martini presentation

- Ask your prospects, "Would you like to give it a go?" Moving towards a positive decision at the end of the presentation, the close is the most important part of the process. If you don't ask, "Would you like to give it a go?" it does not matter how well you conducted your meeting.

If they say yes, arrange a get-together in the next 48 hours.

If they say no, thank them and ask, "Who do you know that might benefit from this?"

In either case, make sure they do not go home empty-handed!

4. The internet and your hosted web site

These are a quick way to get a prospect to review the business, which you can use face-to-face or at a distance.

It is effective for a few reasons:

- It is a very non-threatening approach for your prospect
- It is more time effective
- You are not the issue
- They can see the support that's available.

Explain how the money works (do the Martini presentation) and how this can benefit them.

5. DVD and Audio Presentation

The DVD (*What's it all About?/Business of the 21st Century* – R. *Kiyosaki*) presentation is a great way to share the business with busy people, professionals, cold prospects, etc.

They work well because people do not need to take lots of time out of their lives to hear about the business. The audio message is powerful because they can listen to it when they're driving (and there is no more dead time than driving time!).

Many sceptical people are totally turned around after reviewing the DVD or listening to the audio message. If it interests them, they can listen to it or watch it over and over again.

The DVD is also an excellent tool for a prospect's second exposure to the business, if they've already been to a home meeting, one-on-one, or COP.

The DVD can be an incredibly effective use of your time. Give them out and you can have loads of presentations happening and working for you simultaneously!

They are also a great way to show the business long-distance.

The follow-up

This is where you make money.

Most of the time, what separates the 'I will be,' from the 'I want to be,' can be directly attributed to their willingness and ability to follow up – consistently.

Once you have worked your way through your contact list, you will be left with six scenarios:

1. People you tried, but couldn't get in touch with.

Put these people on a daily follow-up list and discipline yourself to make just three follow-up calls a day. This will take no more than a few minutes in the nooks and crannies of the day. There is no excuse that you haven't got time!

Or send them a 'priority' package with a CD (*UK's Best Kept Secret*) or DVD (*What's it all About?*), *The Independence* newspaper and a brief note asking them to please review the information and call you back asap.

2. People you contact, and invite to meet and who say no.

If the person refuses to meet with you, ask them this: *"John, I understand how busy you are, especially in these uncertain economic times, but before you make any decision, will you take just 15 minutes to listen to a CD/watch a short DVD that might give you a better idea of what it's all about?"*

If they still say no, say: *"Would it be OK if I keep in touch and keep you updated as to what's happening with the company?"*

Then every 10-12 weeks, send them any positive or exciting new information with a little post-it note saying, 'keeping you updated'. Our business is full of successful people who said no, sometimes more than once!

3. People you arrange to meet, and who don't turn up.

When this happens – and it will – you need to call the person, ask if everything is OK and tell them, in an up-beat tone, what they missed. At this point, they will probably apologise. Tell them it's OK, but you need to meet up with them asap.

It is important that you come from a point of strength. Do not get angry, but do stress your time is valuable as well, and you would welcome a call if something comes up before your re-arranged meeting.

4. The contact does not join but gives you referrals.

There are only two ways you can increase your business: find new prospects; or obtain more contacts from the people you know.

A referral is so much more powerful than a cold call because it makes you more credible. But no one volunteers referrals; you must ask for them

5. The contact does not join, but becomes a customer.

This is a good source of referrals. Example: *"John, I have a favour to ask. With my business, my most valued resource is the customer. My priority is knowing you are happy and* satisfied with your decision to be a customer. May I ask, who do you know who would be interested is saving or making money? Do you have three names that come to mind, people who would enjoy the same benefits as you?"

6. The contact becomes a Distributor.

Another good source of referrals! Example: *"Mary, I have a favour to ask. We work our business through word of mouth. Who do you know who would like to earn more money this year than last year? Do you have three names that come to mind of people who would benefit from an extra income stream?"*

And finally: when you sign a new Distributor, remember that they will do what you do, not what you say.

Long distance

You don't need to be local to be successful. You can present the business opportunity, and build a big team, with people who are a long way away from you geographically.

As with the rest of your business, it needs attention, and consistent effort.

How to recruit and sponsor long-distance

These are the basic principles:

- Become a satisfied customer

- Contact and invite by telephone

- Send some recruiting information and/or direct people to your website

- If they are interested, explain how the money works – you can do the Martini presentation over the phone – and sign them up. They can do this online, through your website

- Get them to go to a local COP. If you cannot attend yourself, find out who is hosting the COP, and tell your new Distributor to introduce themselves to the host.

Stay in daily contact with them by phone. This is important!

- You can help them understand the business, by phone

- You can team up with your sponsor and talk them through how to do it by phone, using three-way calling

- Soon enough they will be able to do it without your help, but with the help of the other support systems (trainings, COPs, events).

If you travel to their area, get a commitment over the phone:

- To be available to meet when you are there

- Make sure they become a customer themselves

- Make sure they start their list

- Teach them how to contact and invite, how to show the Martini presentation, and how to share the benefits of the services.

Keep them exposed to the business:

- Arrange to meet them at a big event

- Conduct a three-way call with them and your active up-line

- Make sure they understand the value of massive action for the first 90 days

- Create a sense of urgency within them. What might they lose if they do not work the business?

All of this you can do at a distance, and by phone. It may appear harder at first, but get used to it and it will become natural for you.

How to explode your business

I want to share something special with you about working long-distance. It can open your team up, and boost your business more than you could have imagined.

- Teach your team to send out just one long-distance pack each week. That's a pack with a covering letter, a DVD or CD, a Sales Brochure, and an *Independence* newspaper

- Teach them to send it to an open-minded or smart person they know who lives more than 50 miles from them

- Send it Special Delivery for the greatest impact

- They must commit to sending just one pack per week. No more, no less. But they must do it. No excuses

- Teach every single person in your team to do the same

- Do it yourself: people will do what you do

- Start this habit early. Create momentum.

This method will mean that you start leveraging your team's contacts. If you have just 50 people in your team, that will be 200 long-distance packs going out every single month.

Or to put it another way, that's 2,400 packs going out every year – to people all over the UK, who your team will then teach to do the same.

Imagine the impact of that.

Building and leading your team

Once you have a team – which starts when you have just one
Distributor in your downline – you need to lead and motivate
them.

Promote meetings and events

Promoting and attending events is a key ingredient if you want
to build a large profitable team.

I was taught that if you want to be successful in Network
Marketing, you should get good at three skills – Master the
invite and teach your team to do the same.

1. Get good at showing and teaching the benefits of the
    services

2. Get good at getting in front of people and showing and
    teaching the benefits of the business opportunity

3. (and this is the big one) Get superb at promoting and
    attending events.

The third skill is one of the highest paying, and yet it is
probably the least understood by new Distributors.

Promoting events accelerates your business because it shows
your new Distributors the 'big picture', and helps them
become passionate about their business. It would be great if
people caught the vision of the business when they first join
but, unfortunately, that's not usually the case.

Many, many times, I have seen what happens when Distributors who have been slowly getting going in the business for months go to a big event like a Kick-Off seminar, Massive Action Day (known as MAD) or Express Day, which is the biggest event of all. When they go to these events, they get a 1000-watt light bulb moment.

They get it.

And as a consequence, they take the opportunity a lot more seriously, and really get started at building their business.

I had a very talented Financial Adviser in my business. He had the contacts and the talent, but I just couldn't get him going. He had a bit of an ego problem.

After a great deal of coercing and cajoling on my part, I managed to get him to a Company event that we call Massive Action Day, or MAD.

As the day progressed, one of the testimonials he listened to was by a former colleague of his. The ex-colleague told his story and described how he had progressed through our business. He said that he had now left the finance industry, with all its regulatory issues and in-house politics and problems, and he was happier now with his life than he had been in a long time.

The light bulb finally came on in my Distributor's head. And my word, was he angry because he had wasted a year before he got going with this! He was on fire after that event.

He became more teachable and coachable. And he is a Group Leader at present and will soon be a Senior Group Leader.

You never know what might switch on someone's light. But don't be weak at promoting events. It's up to you to promote them like there's no tomorrow.

Tell your team that it will advance their business by three months if they attend the event. Create a sense of urgency. Create a fear of loss, so your Distributors will make the effort because they don't want to miss out.

Getting the big picture is everything.

Until the vision of the business is in someone's head, it won't be properly in their heart. And if it's not in their heart, they won't be able speak to people with true commitment and enthusiasm.

Make sure you're excited by your team

In the beginning, I wanted the business more for my team than they wanted it for themselves. They didn't excite me.

I was working 12-hour shifts at Manchester airport. I would take a change of clothes with me, and as soon as my shift finished, I would change, ram some food down my mouth and then rush off so I could get straight to the Career Opportunity Presentation. I would get really frustrated when my team didn't make the effort, or didn't attend the meetings.

I came to the conclusion that I had the wrong team.

Sometimes you have to start over. Ouch! But sometimes you need to start afresh. Most of my colleagues who have gone to the top in our business have started over, sometimes more than once. They have had people board but just not the right people. They had to start over to get people who motivated them.

If you need to start over and bring in new people your team will be better for it, you will have learned something new, and your attitude and skill levels will have improved. There will be no more messing around with team members who are acting like they want to be successful, but aren't willing to do the work.

Instead, you will be able to devote yourself entirely to people who will work to build their business – and yours.

Lead your team to success

Leadership is key in developing a dynamic team. The role of the leader is many things, and it changes from day to day. How you lead the way for your team is up to you. Don't get bogged down or overwhelmed by the thought of leadership; it really can come quite easily.

Encourage and teach your team members to plug into the system; to go to training sessions and events, to read books, to listen to CDs and to associate with successful people. Do this, and you are leading whether you realise it or not.

Most importantly, your team will do what you do. So work your business exactly the way you want your team to work their business.

Here are some Golden Rules for leadership:

1. **A leader must have a goal larger than those they lead**. One of the biggest mistakes most people make in our business is that they don't envision the true potential of the business that they are in. The downline team is always looking up for 'big picture' vision and leadership.
2. **A leader is a student of commitment to personal growth**. Stagnation is a killer. Many people think they are at a standstill in life, but you are not; you are either moving forward or you're going backward. A programme for personal growth should be high on your priority list.
3. **A leader is a decision maker.** I learnt a long time ago that a leader is motivated by doing the right thing, while a manager concerns themselves with doing things right. Not all of your decisions will be correct, but it is important to make decisions.
4. **A leader sets the example by being out in front**. True leaders say 'follow me'. This is a business that requires leaders to stand up and be counted.
5. **A leader must have an attitude superior to those they lead.** A leader feeds their mind every day with positive information through books and CDs. A leader focuses on the solutions to the problem, not the problem itself. Negative attitudes are quite damaging and have an impact on the team. One negative statement about the

business or services can stop your team in its tracks, as it shows that the leader is not acting correctly toward the business.

6. **Leadership is about being in contact.** Staying in constant communication with your team members will strengthen your relationship with hem, and motivate them to achieve. Technology has made it so easy to stay in regular contact with all your team and new team members. But if they're new, don't try to communicate in three hours everything you have learned over the last 12 months! If you do that, don't be surprised if a lot of your new Distributors feel overwhelmed.

7. **Leadership is in your activity, and what you do when no one is watching.** It is doing what you said you would do, long after the mood in which you said it has passed.

8. **Pass on leadership; see, do and teach it.**

If other people can do this, so can you

Don't you dare tell me that you can't.

If I can make this business a success, **so can you.**

Throughout my life I have had people tell me, "You can't do that". I grew up on that rough council estate and, like many, I was influenced by my environment. For years and years I thought that people who owned a 'private house' were better than us. No-one I knew owned their own property.

We can be seduced into believing that certain things are beyond us. If no one in your family has worked for themselves or owned a business, some of them might think you are getting above your station and you can't do this business.

The Association that I talked about earlier in this book will be a big influence on whether you sink or swim. Get yourself around the people who can advise and encourage you.

You need to develop an attitude if you are going to swim against the current of mediocrity.

There is a small minority of people you know who might want you to fail, just so they can say, "I told you that wouldn't work."

Even with this book, I had people say to me, "No chance." That was like waving a red rag to a rhino with me (I know it should be a bull, but when you picture a rhino, it's like an unstoppable force!). I was determined to show them they were wrong.

If you don't put the effort in you won't get anything back.

I won't lie to you; there were many times I thought of giving up this business. It took some courage to keep going.

It was Jeff Olson's book and CD set, *The Slight Edge*, that changed my thinking. Just keep doing on a daily basis the little disciplines that seem to make no difference in that moment in time, but whose compounded effect, over time, makes all the difference.

I am so glad I carried on. I am entering my 55th year on this planet. I drew my line in the sand at 43, and if I can make this business a success, so can you.

The Network marketing industry will continue to gain acceptance and grow in strength in the business world and consumer marketplace. Lower cost technology and communications have made starting a home-based business so much easier than ever before, with a much greater chance of becoming successful.

I have seen the shift from the traditional product-based Network Marketing companies to the service-based companies attract more people to the industry than ever before.

Telecom Plus is at the forefront of this revolution.

I believe the economic downturn over the last few years will have a far-reaching effect on our children and, possibly, our children's children. The security once offered by the government – no matter who's in power – and large multinational companies will continue to dissolve. Global competition will force companies to engage in downsizing. All of this creates a big risk for employees who think they have job security.

Faced with the burden of an aging population, I believe we will see a scaling back of the 'social safety nets', leaving hundreds of thousands of UK citizens up the creek.

We are creating a movement of people who take responsibility for their future, who display self-reliance and individual initiative. Our business will inspire many people to take charge of their life, and I want to affirm the ethics of a business in which people succeed by helping others to succeed.

We were once called a nation of shop-keepers. The Great British entrepreneurial spirit will return the entrepreneur who works hard, and dreams big.

There is no greater pleasure than the pleasure of owning your future. I have met literally hundreds of people whose life has been positively **IMPACTED** by this business.

If you work hard and don't quit, that's what this business can do for you.

What it takes to succeed

Whatever you do, you need courage. Whatever course you decide upon, there is always someone to tell you you're wrong.

The tale of two lions

A Zulu warrior is teaching his sons about life. He tells them that there is a terrible battle going on inside him, a battle between two lions.

One is the Lion of courage, hope, determination, love and strength.

The other is the Lion of fear, uncertainty, worry, lethargy and doubt.

The elder son thinks about it for a moment and asks, "Which lion wins?"

The warrior replies, "The one you feed."

Say this to yourself:

I will persist until I succeed.

I was not delivered into this world in defeat.

Nor does failure course in my veins.

I am not a sheep waiting to be prodded by my shepherd.

I am a lion and I refuse to talk, walk or sleep with the sheep.

I will hear not those who weep and complain, for their disease is contagious.

Let them join the sheep.

The slaughterhouse of failure is not my destiny.

Say this to yourself:

Do what others won't do and you will have what others will never have.

The Impact System™

In the first part of this book, I talked about the kind of mindset you need to succeed in this business. I wanted to show how, with the right attitude, you can achieve that mindset, no matter who you are.

In the second part of this book, I have shown you how to make sure that you, as a new Distributor, start your business in the right way. You build a list of 100 plus people you know by name, and you start from there.

Follow the Impact System™, consistently, and you will succeed.

At the start of Part Two, I also showed you the power of leveraging time in building a team. I showed you how you could build a team of over 4,000 Distributors in a year.

You might think that sounds like a perfect scenario that no-one could ever achieve in reality.

But think again.

That team of over 4,000 Distributors was built on you introducing just one person each month, and on them doing the same. In other words, from each person's list of 100 people, you can build a huge business with a success rate of about one in ten.

Does that sound so hard?

Always remember that the best way to teach is by example: people will do what you do.

Follow the Impact System™, and teach the people you sponsor to follow the Impact System™ too.

The Impact System™ has been my route to success, and it can be yours too.

Now it's up to you.

Suggested reading and listening

You don't need to read all of these before you start. In fact, don't – get started!

But as you work on your business, you can keep working on yourself as well. These are some of the books and CDs I have found most useful.

Reading

How to Win Friends and Influence People, by Dale Carnegie.

Think and Grow Rich, by Napoleon Hill.

Being the Best You can Be in MLM, by John Kalench

Communicate to Win, by Richard Denny.

The One Minute Manager, by Kenneth Blanchard and Spencer Johnson

Rich Dad Poor Dad, by Robert Kiyosaki

Business of the 21st Century, by Robert Kiyosaki.

Listening

Go for No, by Richard Fenton and Andrea Waltz.

Making the shift, by Darren Hardy.

Business of the 21st Century, by Robert Kiyosaki.

The Slight Edge, by Jeff Olson.

Questions are the answers, by Allan Pease.

Building your NWM business, by Jim Rohn.

Goals; Don't just Dream it, Do it, by Chris Williams.

Anything, www.fortunenow.com , by Tom Shreiter

Don't quit

I often say there are only two ways you won't succeed at this business. One is not to join. The other is to quit. You've joined, so now make sure you don't quit.

When things go wrong, as they sometimes will,
When the road you're trudging seems all uphill,
When the funds are low and the debts are high,
And you want to smile, but you have to sigh,
When care is pressing you down a bit,
Rest if you must, but don't you quit.

Life is queer with its twists and turns,
As every one of us sometimes learns,
And many a failure turns about
When they might have won, had they stuck it out.
Don't give up though the pace seems slow,
You may succeed with another blow.

Often the struggler has given up
When he might have captured the victor's cup;
And he learned too late when the night came down,
How close he was to the golden crown.

Success is failure turned inside out
The silver tint of the clouds of doubt
And you never can tell how close you are,
It may be near when it seems so far.
So stick to the fight when you're hardest hit,
It's when things seem worst that you must not quit!

Think of me as a nagging voice in your ear.

You might be stuck on the hamster wheel of life, in a job that doesn't give you a spark any more. You might be a person who has never been given the chance to work for themselves, or a person who wants more out of life and is willing to get it. You might be a person who is sick and tired of being sick and tired.

I love this Arabic saying that a friend of mine shared with me years ago; "Don't wait until you are thirsty before you start digging your well".

At many presentations you will hear me say, "Don't think what if this doesn't work for you, but what if it does work for you? What could this business help you achieve if you stick with it?"

Why not you and why not now? If we can, so can YOU.

And whatever you do, **don't quit.**

In closing

If this book has helped you, please give it to someone else, or tell them about it.

If you have any stories or information that you would like to share, I would welcome the opportunity to share them with other readers in the future.

Thanks

Contact me at

stephan@longworth.go-plus.net or

www.StephanLongworth.com

Lightning Source UK Ltd.
Milton Keynes UK
UKOW06f1215030816

279838UK00002B/70/P